BEST BABY NAMES FOR BOYS

THE **nameberry** GUIDE

BEST BABY NAMES FOR BOYS

Linda Rosenkrantz & Pamela Redmond Satran

INTRODUCTION

Why buy a baby name book in this era of more and free and better name information online?

Indeed, every name in this book, along with our trademark information about it, is available on **Nameberry**, the website that encompasses everything we've written about names in our ten bestselling books.

But what you'll get with this book, what you can't find on our site or anywhere else, is our personal curation of the best choices for boys from the enormous universe of names. There are nearly 20,000 boys' names on Nameberry. In this book, we've winnowed that down to the 600 most appealing, most usable, all around best boys' names.

By picking the best names for you, we make it easier for you to pick the best name for your baby. This is the book that you'll curl up in bed with at night, that you'll discuss over dinner with your partner, that is most likely to be the source of the name you'll ultimately choose for your son.

The 600 best names here are drawn from a wide range of styles and choices:

- **Classic Boys' Names** — Included here are the most enduring boys' classics, from biblical names ranging from Abel to Zachary, traditional choices from Arthur to William, and ancient names from Alexander to Xavier, all with detailed information on their history and current appeal.
- **Stylish Names for Boys** — Which popular and trending names will transcend the moment and prove lasting choices? We include picks from the top of the pops, such as Liam and Owen, and highlight cool choices that fit in with current styles but stand further from the spotlight: Booker and Lennox, for instance.
- **Adventurous Names** — What are the most usable unusual names? You'll find hundreds of unique choices here for your son, from revived classics like Cassius and Montgomery to international ideas such as Laszlo and Soren to nontraditional first names including Basie and Baz, Drummer and Zephyr.

All the names here link back to Nameberry, making it easy for you to explore more about your favorites: You can track down which lists include the names you like best (or create your own lists around them), read blog posts about them, see what people have to say about them on the forums, and maybe use them as jumping off points to find other choices you like even better, beyond the 600 here.

We believe this book will be the centerpiece for your conversations and process of choosing a name for your baby boy. It's the perfect place to start, the central point from which to explore, and the place you'll likely end your journey, with your choice of the very best of the best.

A

Aaron

Hebrew, "high mountain; exalted, enlightened"

Aaron has been in and around the Top 50 for two decades, and is still an attractive, timeless, choice; the softness of Aaron's initial double vowel gives it an appealing gentleness.

In the Old Testament, Aaron, the older brother of Moses who was appointed by God to be his brother's spokesman, was the first High Priest of the Israelites.

Notable namesakes include Aaron Burr and composer Aaron Copland — and currently, Aaron Eckhart and Aaron Paul. Aaron has appeared in works by Shakespeare, James Fenimore Cooper and George Eliot.

Elvis's middle name was spelled Aron, one of several variant spellings, which also include Arron and Arun. The Hebrew version is Aharon; in Yiddish it can be Aaran, and the name appears in Arabic as Haroun or Harun.

There are plants known as Aaron's Rod and Aaron's Beard.

Abbott

Hebrew, Aramaic, "father"

Abbott is a neglected masculine surname with religious overtones as the head of a monastery. Though the feminine nickname Abby could be a slight drawback, Abbott is still an attractive offbeat possibility.

The political activist and co-founder of the Yippies, Abbie Hoffman's birth name was Abbott.

Abbot (one "t") Kinney is known for developing Venice, California — whose main thoroughfare bears his name.

Abel

Hebrew, "breath"

Abel, the name of Adam and Eve's unfortunate younger son, compensates with positive connotations: capable, competent, ready and willing.

Abel has literary connections to the novels of Dickens and Trollope, and is also one of the few well-known Old Testament names not plagued by overuse. Having been chosen for their second son by Amy Poehler and Will Arnett could give it a real popularity bounce.

Abel's ranking at Number 192 on the Most Popular list — the highest it has been since records have been kept — could be due to its popularity in the Hispanic community, where it is pronounced ah-BELL, as it is in France.

Abel's namesakes include two movie directors, Abel Gance and Abel Ferrara.

Abelard

German, "noble, steadfast"
Abelard brings to mind Peter/Pierre Abelard, the great twelfth-century Breton scholastic philosopher and theologian, who was equally celebrated for his tragic love affair with Heloise — one of the world's most famous love stories.

This highly unusual name just might appeal to the fearless baby namer.

Abijah

Hebrew, "God is my father"
Abijah is a truly unusual, truly unisex, truly appealing biblical name. There were several male Abijahs in the Bible; one of them, known as Abijah of Judah, was the fourth king of the House of David, and also a couple of females.

A Colonial era favorite with an energetic, modern aura, Abijah is a possible Elijah replacement. A short form found in historical records: Bige, though Abe can work too.

Abner

Hebrew, "father of light."
This neglected biblical name — it was the name of the commander of Saul's army and appears twice in the New Testament — is ready to flee Dogpatch. It was regularly used in the nineteenth century, but was pretty much demolished by the long-running hillbilly comic strip L'il Abner, which began in 1934 and ran through 1977. A more respectable namesake is Abner Doubleday, who has been credited with inventing baseball.

Abner also has literary credentials, having appeared in works by James Fenimore Cooper, Thomas Hardy and Eugene O'Neill.

Abraham

Hebrew, "father of multitudes"
Abraham was the first of the Old Testament patriarchs and is considered the founding father of the Jewish people. He was originally named Abram, until, according to Genesis,

he was told "No longer shall your name be Abram, but your name shall be Abraham, for I have made you the father of a multitude of nations."

In the nineteenth century, President Lincoln hung a beard on the name, which kept it from reaching the mass modern popularity of other biblical names like Benjamin and Samuel.

Now that names like Ezekiel and Isaiah are making a comeback, more parents are thinking about a Baby Abie, or — even better — a Baby Bram, to the point where Abraham now ranks at Number 194. And it does, of course, have the noble namesake of Honest Abe to recommend it.

Country music singer Lila McCann chose it for her son, as did musician Ziggy Marley.

Abraham Van Helsing is the wise Dutch doctor in *Dracula* who understands the ways of vampires.

Abraxas

Persian mythological name

Abraxas is a sci-fi-sounding name with earthly possibilities, but some playground challenges.

Abraxas has a long and convoluted history, dating back to ancient Egyptian mythology and the Gnostics who worshiped him as the Supreme Being. The name Abraxas was carved on antique gemstones that were used as charms.

Abraxas lives on in modern pop culture, as the name of the musical group Santana's second album, in *Harry Potter and the Half-Blood Prince* as Draco's grandfather, on several TV series and video games, and as a cosmic entity in Marvel Comics.

Trivia note: Abracadabra was based on Abraxas.

A unique name with powerful vibes!

Absalom

Hebrew, "father of peace"

Absalom, because of its biblical and literary associations, just might appeal to the daring namegiver.

In the Old Testament, Absalom was the handsome, favored but rebellious son of King David. In literature, Absalom appears in Chaucer's *The Canterbury Tales*, as the repeated title of a Faulkner novel — which refers to the biblical personage rather than the name of a character — in the novel *Cry, the Beloved Country*; and, on a more trivial note, as the name of the caterpillar in the Tim Burton version of *Alice in Wonderland*.

The growing-in-popularity Axel is the Scandinavian form of the name.

Ace

Latin, "one, unity"

No longer tied to the hapless Ace Ventura, this jaunty, high-flying nickname name is starting to take flight among celebrity and other parents, with its nothing but positive references to doing well in tests and poker games, on the tennis court and golf course, and in the air.

Jessica Simpson, Natalie Appleton, Tom Dumont and Jennie Finch all have little Aces. The best known grownup with the name is Ace Frehley, born Paul, onetime KISS guitarist.

Adair

Scottish and Irish, "oak tree ford"

Adair has flair, the grace of a Fred Astaire. It's a Scottish surname which came from the first name Edgar.

In recent years, it has also been used for girls.

Adlai

Hebrew, "my adornment" or "God is just"

Adlai is an Old Testament name long associated with 1950s liberal presidential candidate Stevenson, who was named after his grandfather, who was Grover Cleveland's vice president in the nineteenth century. Now it's an unusual biblical choice ripe for rediscovery.

In the Bible, Adlai was a minor character, the father of one of King David's herdsmen. Adlai is a contracted form of the Hebrew name Adaliah.

Alaric

German, "all-powerful ruler"

Alaric is an ancient regal name that sounds modern enough to be considered. Alaric was a traditional name for the kings of the Ostrogoths, the most famous of whom was Alaric I, the King of the West Goths who sacked Rome in 410.

In literature, Alaric was a noble character in P. G. Wodehouse's *Blandings Castle* novels, the lead character in Alexander Theroux's *Darconville's Cat*, appeared in Stephen King's *The Dark Tower* series, and is the name of a history teacher on *The Vampire Diaries*.

More unusual than Frederic or Roderic, Alaric could make a quaintly quirky path to all the Al and Rick nicknames.

Alcott

English, "dweller at the old cottage"

Alcott evokes shades of nineteenth-century New England, and memories of the author of the books *Little Women* and *Little Men*. Louisa May Alcott was the daughter of Amos Bronson Alcott, noted educator, writer and philosopher, and colleague of Ralph Waldo Emerson and Henry David Thoreau.

Alcott would make an unusual and interesting surname name choice.

Alec

Diminutive of Alexander, Greek, "defending warrior"

Alec, though an old nickname for Alexander, is much fresher sounding than Alex, with the additional advantage of not being unisex — there are as many girl Alexes these days as there are boys.

Alec Baldwin is by far the best known current bearer of the name; in the past, there have been actor Alec Guinness and writer Alec Waugh.

Alessandro

Italian variation of Alexander, "defending men"

For anyone seeking a more exotic and unusual version of Alexander, this is a real winner.

Notable namesakes include the great Italian opera composer Scarlatti and the influential physicist Alessandro Volta, known primarily for the invention of the battery you use every day — as well as the contemporary hunky actor Alessandro Nivola.

Appealing short forms are Alessio and Sandro (as in Botticelli).

Alexander

Greek, "defending men"

Alexander has been in the Top 25 since 1991, and is still at a high Number 9. The noble Alexander has led to the popularity of so many spin-offs, such as Alex, Zander, Xan and Zan — not to mention all the female versions — that it almost feels as if the name world's been Alextrified out. But namers are still attracted to its imposing historic pedigree.

According to Greek legend, the first Alexander was Paris, who was given the nickname Alexander by the shepherds whose flocks he defended against robbers, followed by Alexander the Great, aka Alexander III, who conquered much of Asia. A royal name in Scotland, it is still highly popular there. In Gaelic, the name became Alasdair, in Spain Alejandro, and in Italy Alessandro.

Among the many notable Alexanders in history, stand-outs are Hamilton, Graham Bell, Fleming, Pope and Haig.

Naomi Watts and Liev Schreiber's Alexander is known as Sasha.

Alfie

Diminutive of Alfred, English, "wise counselor"

Alfie is the seventh most popular boys' name in England and Wales, where retro nickname names are ultratrendy, but it hasn't really been picked up on in the U.S.

Thanks to some louche fictional characters, Alfie has long had a sexy, flirtatious image. First there was the Michael Caine character in the 1966 eponymous film, followed by a 2004 remake starring Jude Law. In Britain, the name was given a big boost by the Alfie Moon character in the long-running soap, *EastEnders*. There have been several Alfie songs as well, most recently one by Lily Allen written for her little brother.

Both Alfie and cousin Archie are spunky nickname possibilities, with a bit of an English accent.

Alfred

English, "wise counselor"

Alfred is up off his recliner! If you're looking for a path to Fred, you can go directly to Frederick or take the long way round with the so-far-out-it's-in-again Alfred.

Alfred the Great, King of Wessex (called "England's darling") was a wise, compassionate and scholarly king of old England, in the tenth century. His name reached the height of its popularity from the late eighteenth to the early twentieth century — it was in the Top 50 in the US until 1932.

Hipper nicknames: Alf, Alfie and Fred.

Alistair

English spelling of Alasdair, Scottish version of Alexander, "defending warrior"

With many British names invading the Yankee name pool, the sophisticated Alistair could and should be part of the next wave. You have a triple choice with this name — the British spell it Alistair or Alastair, while the Scots prefer Alasdair — but they're all suave Gaelic versions of Alexander. Adopted by the lowland Scots by the seventeenth century, the name didn't become popular outside Scotland and Ireland until the twentieth century.

Both Andrew Lloyd Weber and Rod Stewart chose the Alastair spelling for their sons' names.

Alonzo

Italian diminutive of Alphonso, "noble, ready"

Alonzo is dashing and debonair, with a large measure of Latin flair.

You may be surprised to know that Alonzo has been on the Most Popular list since 1880, when such records began to be kept, at which point it was Number 110. The same is true for nickname Lon, which was 193 at the time.

Alonso Quijano was the real name of Don Quixote — Alonso being the Spanish version of the name. In the old Judy Garland musical *Meet Me in St. Louis*, Alonzo/Lon was the name of both her father and brother.

Horror film star Lon Chaney was christened Alonso, but Lon Chaney, Jr was Creighton at birth. Alonzo Mourning is a former basketball star who goes by the nickname Zo — much more modern sounding than Lon or Lonnie.

Amadeus

Latin, "lover of God"

Wolfgang Amadeus Mozart's middle name could make an interesting pick for music-loving parents — if only in middle place. *Amadeus* was the title of a Peter Shaffer play which became an award-winning film in 1984.

German-born tennis ace Boris Becker chose Amadeus for the name of his fourth son.

Ambrose

Latin, "immortal one"

A favorite of British novelists including Evelyn Waugh and P. G. Wodehouse, Ambrose has an air of blooming well-being and upper-class erudition. It comes from the same Greek root as "ambrosia," the food of the gods, literally "belonging to the immortals."

Ambrose was the name of one of the important doctors of the early Christian church, the fourth-century St. Ambrose. It also belonged to one of the four great Latin teachers of Christianity, who also developed the use of music in church services. TV fanatics might be interested to know that in 1961, Ambrose was designated the patron saint of educational television by Pope John XXII.

Ambrose's only problem is finding a nickname — aside from the all too obvious Rosie.

Amias

Latin, "loved"

Amias or Amyas is an obscure name with an attractive sound and feel and a lovely meaning. Though it might sound like a biblical name, it is not, but is a surname that may be related to Amadeus or even be a male version of Amy — which would make it one of the few boys' names to be derived from a girls'.

The Amyas version became known via the hero of the mega-popular 1855 Charles Kingsley novel, *Westward Ho!*, Captain Sir Amyas Leigh.

Amos

Hebrew, "carried by God"

Amos has been shunned since the 1930s due to its association with racially stereotyped characters on the radio and TV show *Amos 'n' Andy*, but we think it's time to move beyond that dated image and reconsider this robust biblical name.

Amos was an eighth-century (BCE) prophet whose sayings are collected in the biblical Book named after him, and the name was popular among the Puritans.

There are characters named Amos in novels by George Eliot and Thomas Hardy, and its most famous contemporary bearer is Israeli author Amos Oz. The name has also been associated with Famous Amos cookies, a company founded by Wally Amos.

Anderson

Scandinavian, "son of Anders"

Anderson has been shooting up in popularity, no doubt in large part due to the prominence of white-haired cable newsman Anderson Cooper, son of Gloria Vanderbilt. Perhaps surprisingly though, Anderson was even higher on the list in 1880.

Angus

Gaelic, "one strength"

Angus is rapidly moving from fuddy-duddy, kilt-wearing old Scotsman to hip young American; it's definitely a plausible choice, particularly for parents whose roots go back to Glasgow. The ancient Celtic form Oenghus has important historical overtones in Scotland, and the Gaelic form Aonghas is associated with two distinguished modern poets. In Irish folklore, Angus Og is a chieftain-lord who used his magical powers and treasures for the pleasure and prosperity of mankind.

These days, Angus is even more popular in Australia than Scotland, possibly due to the fame of Scottish-born Australian musician Angus Young, lead guitarist and co-founder of the seminal rock band AC/DC.

Other pop culture references: Angus was the first name of TV's *MacGyver* and the young actor who plays the half man on *Two and a Half Men* is Angus T. Jones. Angus Wilson was a noted British novelist and short story writer.

Ansel

German, "with divine protection" or "follower of a nobleman"

Ansel, primarily associated with the great western photographer Ansel Adams, famed for his magnificent photographs of the Yosemite Valley, could make a creative artist-hero choice. For Adams it was a family name — he was named after his uncle, Ansel Easton.

Derived from the same root as Anselm (another possibility), Ansel is a medieval Germanic name, whose meaning is somewhat unclear.

Ansel has been far from a unique name — it was on and off the popularity lists in the late nineteenth and early twentieth centuries, reaching as high as Number 540 in 1893.

Apollo

Greek mythology name

With mythological names rising, the handsome son of Zeus and god of medicine, music, and poetry among many other things might offer an interesting, if high-pressure, option. But if Romeo and Venus are now deemed baby-appropriate, why not Apollo? Olympic speed skater Apolo Anton Ohno might inspire some parents.

Other cool associations are to NASA's Apollo program, from 1961-72, that succeeded in landing the first humans on the moon when astronauts Neil Armstrong and Buzz Aldrin landed their lunar module and walked on the moon's surface; and to the historic Apollo Theatre in Harlem, on whose stage the careers of Billie Holiday, Ella Fitzgerald, Aretha Franklin, Stevie Wonder, the Supremes, the Jackson 5, and countless others were launched.

Aram

Hebrew, "high elevated"

Aram is a popular Armenian name with a pleasing sound that became known in this country through the works of William Saroyan, namely the 1940 book of short stories, *My Name in Aram*, centering on Aram Garoghlanian, a boy of Armenian descent growing up in Fresno, California. Saroyan also named his son Aram.

Aram appears in the Bible as a son of Shem and grandson of Noah; it is also a biblical place name. In addition, Aram is the third day of the month in the Armenian calendar.

A well-known bearer is Aram Khachaturian, the Armenian composer.

Archer

English, "bowman"

Archer is an Anglo-Saxon surname that feels more modern than most because of its on-target occupational and *Hunger Games* associations. And it's a nice way to bypass the clunky Archibald to get to the cool nickname Archie.

But have a look at that amazing popularity chart below: After 1889, Archer took a 130-year nap, resurfacing on the Top 1000 in 2009 and now shooting straight upwards. Two years ago, we named Archer one of our Hottest Names of 2011 — and, indeed, it jumped 103 places that year, thanks in part to Archer's similarity to popular Asher and its cross-gender appeal. Moms may like its literary gentility and dads its tough-guy FX cartoon appeal. Or, of course, vice versa.

Trivia tidbit: Archer is the name of Dr. Doolittle's father.

Archibald

Teutonic, "truly brave"
The short form Archie is so open and friendly — and very trendy in the British Isles — that some parents are now beginning to consider the formerly fusty Archibald as well. Former *SNL* comedians Amy Poehler and Will Arnett are one couple who made this breakthrough choice.

After being introduced to England in the twelfth century, Archibald became especially popular in Scotland, where it was in the Top 20 until the 1930s, but later took on a stuffy, aristocratic air. In the US, Archibald ranked as high as Number 279 in 1889.

A notable literary namesake is poet Archibald MacLeish, and Archibald was the full name of both comic-book star Archie Andrews and curmudgeon Archie Bunker. And of course, suave Cary Grant was born Archibald Alexander Leach.

Archie

Diminutive of Archibald, Teutonic, "truly brave"
Forget Archie Bunker, forget Archie comics, and take a fresh look at this amiably retro nickname name. It's made a big comeback in the U.K. — where it's now in the Top 20 — and seems destined for stardom here too now that it's been chosen by funny couple Amy Poehler and Will Arnett for their young son, though they did put the full name Archibald on the birth certificate.

Archie can be a female nickname name too — Archie Panjabi, who won an Emmy for her role as Kalinda Sharm in *The Good Wife* in 2010, was born Archana.

Ari

Hebrew, diminutive of Ariel, "lion of God"; also Greek, diminutive of Aristotle
This short form of Ariel stands up better as a male name than its progenitor does. It is also short for Aristotle, as in Onassis, and is a prominent character on TV's *Entourage* — the überagent Ari Gold.

Among other prominent bearers have been Ari Fleischer, White House Press Secretary for President George W. Bush and Ari Emanuel, powerful talent agent and possible inspiration for Ari Gold.

Ari Ben Canaan is the main character in the Leon Uris novel *Exodus*, played by Paul Newman on screen and Ari is the name of one of the Tenenbaum sons in *The Royal Tenenbaums*.

Arjun

Hindi, "bright, shining, white"

Popular in India and among Indo-Americans, this name of the hero of a famous Hindu epic has an extremely pleasing sound.

Arjun is based on Arjuna, who was in Indian legend the son of the king of gods, close friend of Lord Krishna, and considered the greatest warrior on earth.

Arlo

Spanish, "barberry tree"

Arlo, strongly associated with shaggy singer Arlo Guthrie, has an animated and cheery feel, thanks to its upbeat "o" ending. Some Arlo lovers these days might be more inspired by *Justified*'s anti-hero Arlo Givens. Arlo was chosen by Toni Collette for her son, which might give it a further bounce in popularity, while Johnny Knoxville nudged Arlo into the unisex column when he used it for his daughter.

Arlo was not such a rarity in the first half of the twentieth century — it was Number 667 in 1915, for example.

Arrow

Word name

Words are not always easy to translate into baby names, but the implications of being straight and swift lend this one great potential as a name. It also has the popular "o"-sound ending, which brings it further into the realm of possibility. Rising rock star Aja Volkman pulled a gender switch when she named her daughter Arrow Eve.

Arthur

Celtic, "bear"

Arthur, once the shining head of the Knights of the Round Table, is, after decades of neglect, now being polished up and restored by some stylish parents.

In addition to his leading role in the Arthurian legends, Arthurs figure prominently in *The Scarlet Letter*, Poe's *The Narrative of Arthur Gordon Pym of Nantucket*, and George Eliot's *Adam Bede*. There are also countless Arthurs in children's literature, movies, and

TV — including The Fonz. Most recently, Arthur was the son of Mr. and Mrs. Santa in the eponymous movie *Arthur Christmas*.

Arthur has many notable namesakes, including playwright Arthur Miller, writer/astronomer Arthur C. Clarke, writers Arthur Conan Doyle, Rimbaud and Koestler, philosopher Schopenhauer, conductor Arthur Fiedler, and tennis great Arthur Ashe, the first African-American to win the U.S. Open. Queen Victoria's seventh child was Prince Arthur.

Arthur was a Top 20 name from at least 1880 through 1926. And in 2011, actress Selma Blair named her son Arthur Saint.

Asa

Hebrew, "doctor, healer"; Japanese, "born in the morning"
A short but strong biblical name with multicultural appeal, Asa is enjoying new visibility thanks to hot young actor Asa Butterfield of *Hugo* fame.

Asa was the name of an important biblical king of Judah, who reigned for more than forty years. In modern times, the name was long associated with the strong patriarch Asa Buchanan on the soap opera *One Life to Live*, but since the character "died" in 2007, this gives the name plenty of room to rejuvenate. Popular with the Puritans, Asa can be found in the novels of James Fenimore Cooper and Theodore Dreiser. A notable real-life namesake is the highly influential botanist Asa Gray, and Asa was the birth name of Al Jolson.

Radiohead's Colin Greenwood has a son named Asa.

Asa could also be a path to the hip nickname Ace or an alternative to the rapidly rising Asher.

Asher

Hebrew, "fortunate, blessed, happy one"
Asher — an excellent, soft and sensitive Old Testament choice — is definitely on the rise, climbing almost one hundred places in the last five years, and a Nameberry biblical favorite. Asher's ascent is especially amazing given that it took a hundred-year hiatus from the Top 1000, from the 1890s until reappearing in the 1990s. And now Asher is close to breaking into the Top 100.

In the Bible, Asher was one of Jacob's twelve sons who gave their names to the tribes of Israel.

Asher has been chosen for their sons by TV newswoman Campbell Brown and actress Embeth Davidtz. Its image was somewhat rejuvenated by an appearance as a character on *Gossip Girl*, and the rapper Asher Roth.

The novel *My Name is Asher Lev* by Chaim Potok is the story of a New York Hasidic Jewish boy with artistic aspirations.

Oh — and another plus for Asher: the handsome diminutive Ash.

Atticus

Latin, "from Attica"

Atticus, with its trendy Roman feel combined with the upstanding, noble image of Atticus Finch in *To Kill a Mockingbird*, is a real winner. In fact, so many people have been inspired by the character embodied by Gregory Peck that Atticus Finch was voted the greatest hero of American film by the American Film Institute.

The name of an important Roman literary figure named for the Greek region around Athens, Atticus has continued to rise in the past two years — up 150 places — and is a firm Nameberry favorite.

Daniel Baldwin and Isabella Hoffman were ahead of the curve when they chose Atticus for their son born in 1996; since then, Summer Phoenix and Casey Affleck named their little boy Atticus, and Tom Dumont made it the middle name for his son Rio.

Auberon

English from German, "noble, bearlike"

Rarely heard in the US, Auberon has a gentle autumnal feel rare in a male name. Possibly starting as a pet form of Aubrey, it was also influenced by Oberon, the king of the fairies in Shakespeare's *A Midsummer Night's Dream.*

The most famous bearer of the name is British journalist and critic Auberon Waugh (whose grandfather was Aubrey), of the literary Waugh clan.

The Oberon spelling is another recommended option.

Auden

English, "old friend"

The poetic, soft-spoken Auden has recently started to be considered as a first name option, used for both sexes, appreciated for its pleasing sound as well as its link to the distinguished modern Anglo-American poet W.H. Auden.

August

German form of Latin Augustus, "majestic, venerable"

August has been heating up in Hollywood — used by Mariska Hargitay, Lena Olin, Dave Matthews and Jeanne Tripplehorn, (and by Garth Brooks for his daughter), and is rapidly becoming the preferred month of the year for boys. The month of August was named after the Emperor Augustus.

August has two august literary namesakes: the Swedish playwright August Strindberg (it has always been a popular name in Scandinavia), and August Wilson, as well as photographer August Sander.

The French version is Auguste (ow-GOOST), as in Edgar Allan Poe's clever detective Auguste Dupin and famed sculptor Auguste Rodin.

Augustine

English variation of Augustus, "majestic, venerable"

Augustine is more substantial (and saintly) than August, less august than Augustus, and, along with its nickname Gus, is definitely a viable choice.

Augustine is actually the diminutive form of Augustus, and achieved its fame via the great fourth-century saint, St. Augustine of Hippo, whose teachings and writings had a great effect on early Christianity.

A major character in *Uncle Tom's Cabin* is Augustine St. Clare. The full name of the author of *Ulysses* and *Finnegan's Wake* is James Augustine Aloysius Joyce.

Model Linda Evangelista chose the French form Augustin for her son, also used by Jerry Hall and Mick Jagger as a middle name for their son James.

The Spanish Agustin is experiencing a wild burst of popularity in South America: in recent years, it has been the Number 1 name in Uruguay, and in the Top 5 in Argentina.

Augustus

Latin, "majestic, venerable"

Parents are beginning to look at imposing, somewhat fusty-sounding names like this one with fresh eyes: they definitely make a strong statement.

Augustus originated as a title given by the Roman Senate to the first Roman Emperor, Octavian, the adopted son of Julius Caesar, in 27 B.C. and adopted by him as a name. In the U.S., Augustus reached a high of Number 175 in 1880, fell off the list in 1970, then made a return appearance in 1991, and is now Number 697

Augustus Snodgrass is a character in Charles Dickens's novel *The Pickwick Papers*, and George Bernard Shaw wrote a play titled *Augustus Does His Bit*. Augustus John was a famed British portrait painter, and Augustus Saint-Gaudens, a well-known sculptor.

No starbaby Augustuses as yet, but Dixie Chick Emily Robson used Augustus as a middle name for her son, and Dan Aykroyd did the same — for his daughter.

The diminutive form, Augustine, is also an interesting option; variant Augustin was used by model Linda Evangelista.

Aurelius

Latin, "the golden one"

Since Aurelius was given the supermodel seal of approval by Elle Macpherson, this is one of the Roman emperor names, like Augustus, now in the realm of possibility. Like the female Aurelia and Aurora, Aurelius has a particularly warm golden aura.

In ancient Roman history, the name is associated with Marcus Aurelius, a Roman Emperor from 161 to 180 AD, the last of the so-called "Five Good Emperors." He is also considered one of the most important Stoic philosophers.

Autry

French surname, "ancient power"

Loose, lean, and lanky cowboy-sounding names have become a recent trend, but how about the name of a real one — the Singing Cowboy Gene. Autry might be thought of as a masculine spin on the fashionable Audrey or a fresher version of Austin or Auden.

Some other cowboy surnames from the Golden Age of movie and TV westerns: Boone, Boyd, Cody, Corrigan, Gibson, Hart, Holt, Houston, McCoy and Renaldo.

Axel

German, "father of peace"; Scandinavian variation of Absalom

Axel is the perfect heavy metal rock name, thanks to Guns N' Roses's Axl Rose (born William). Axel is a popular Scandinavian form of the biblical Absalom, who was a son of King David, and is the name of the title character of William Faulkner's *Absalom, Absalom*.

Growing in popularity, along with a lot of other names featuring the powerful letter "x," Axel is now at Number 160. It entered the popularity list in 1989, one year after the release of one of Guns N' Roses's biggest hits. It is very popular in Scandinavia (as high as Number 15 in Sweden), Germany and France.

Axel was chosen by Will Ferrell for his third son, and also by Rob McElhenney and Kaitlin Olson for their boys, and it's the middle name of Tiger Woods's boy Charlie. Fergie and Josh Duhamel chose the Guns 'N' Roses spelling for their son Axl Jack. Axel Foley was the character played by Eddie Murphy in the *Beverly Hills Cop* movies and, going further back, was the name of an important character in Jules Verne's *Journey to the Center of the Earth*.

Azariah

Hebrew, "helped by God"

Azariah is a rarely used biblical name that moves way beyond Adam and Abraham; its pleasant sound makes it one to watch.

Azariah is actually one of the most common names in the Bible, borne by twenty-three different men, including the head of King Solomon's prefects.

Spelled without the final "h," it is also used for girls.

Aziz

Arabic, "powerful and beloved"

This traditional Arabic name represents one of the 99 attributes of Allah. Colorful and energetic, it was brought into the realm of crossover possibility via the lively personality of Aziz Ansari, stand-up comic and featured actor on *Parks and Recreation*, playing cocky Tom Haverford (born Darwish Sabir Ismael Gani).

The female version Aziza, also has a lot of exotic appeal.

B

Baird

Scottish occupational name, "minstrel, poet"
Meaning bard, this is an original choice with poetic and melodic undertones. Bard itself has also come into consideration, both names bringing to mind Shakespeare and other literary lights.

The Scottish surname Baird's most notable bearer was John Logie Baird, the Scottish engineer and inventor of the Televisor, the world's first practical television system in 1926, and also the world's first fully electronic color TV tube two years later. Some might also remember puppeteers Bil and Cora Baird.

Baker

English occupational surname
One of the most appealing of the newly hip occupational names, evoking sweet smells emanating from the oven. Much fresher sounding than others that have been around for a while, like Cooper and Carter.

We don't know any first-name namesakes, but there are plenty of notable surnamed Bakers, including writers Nicholson and Russell, actor Simon, Senator Howard, rocker Ginger, jazz musician Chet, blues singer Anita, and entertainer Josephine.

Balthazar

Phoenician, "Baal protects the King"
This evocative name of one of the Three Wise Men of the Orient, also spelled Balthasar, may finally be ready for prime time. Balthazar, Melchior and Caspar were the Magi who brought gifts of gold, frankincense and myrrh to the baby Jesus, though their names were not mentioned in the Bible.

Balthazar, in its various spellings, has been attached to a number of distinguished artists, writers and philosophers of the past; the most prominent contemporary bearer is Balthazar Getty, actor and great-grandson of J. Paul Getty. The iconoclastic modern painter Balthus was born Balthasar.

Balthazar is well represented in literature. The name appears in no fewer than four Shakespeare plays, is the title of a Lawrence Durrell novel, is the main character of a Balzac novel, and has been seen in everything from a James Bond film to *Buffy the Vampire Slayer* to The Smurfs to Xbox and online games, and there is a J. P. Donleavy novel titled *The Beastly Beatitudes of Balthazar B.*

Barnaby

English variation of Barnabas, Aramaic, "son of consolation"

Barnaby, a genial and energetic name with an Irish-sounding three-syllable lilt, is an ancient appellation that manages to be both unusual and highly attractive and deserves to be used more than it is. A sweet-spot name that's a real winner.

Barnaby is a version of Barnabas, the name of an Apostle companion of St. Paul on his missionary journeys. The name of the good-natured hero of Dickens's novel *Barnaby Rudge*, it became more familiar to the modern American public through the TV series *Barnaby Jones*. Barnaby has been a character in *Hello, Dolly!*, a doctor played by Cary Grant in the movie *Monkey Business*, a comic strip character, and has starred in a number of children's books.

Bartholomew

Aramaic "son of the furrow"

Bartholomew is an apostle's name that's been out of favor for centuries but might appeal again to the parent in search of an old but rare choice. The challenge could be to avoid the Simpson-ish nickname. That character, by the way, has the full name of Bartholomew JoJo Simpson, and creator Matt Groening came up with Bart as an — uh oh — anagram for brat. Two old alternate nicknames are Barty and Tolly.

Ben Jonson's 1614 comedy *Bartholomew Fair* is set in London on St. Bartholomew's Day. Charles Dickens used the name in *Bleak House*, and, more recently, Bartholomew Cubbins is the protagonist of the Dr. Seuss books *The 500 Hats of Bartholomew Cubbins* and *Bartholomew and the Oobleck*.

Bartleby

English surname, probably related to Bartholomew, "son of the furrow"

Bartleby (that's his last name) the Scrivener is a famous Herman Melville character whose surprisingly powerful refrain was, "I would prefer not to." Or, in the immortal words of any two-year-old: No.

Putting that aside, Bartleby could make a uniquely lively literary alternative to Barnaby.

Bartleby the Scrivener: A Story of Wall Street was made into movies three times, the latest starring Christian Glover. In the 1999 film *Dogma*, Bartleby is a fallen angel played by Ben Affleck.

Basie

Scottish surname, meaning unknown

Basie is a fabulous jazz name to honor the Count, whose birth name was William, the influential pianist, organist, bandleader and composer who led his band for almost fifty years.

There are lots of other jazzy names you might want to consider, including Ellington, Miles, Quincy, Dexter, Mercer, and Bix. Woody Allen named his two daughters after jazz musicians — Bechet for clarinetist Sidney Bechet and Manzie for Manzie Johnson, the drummer in Bechet's band.

Basil

Greek, "regal"

Although Greek in origin — in the fourth century, a bishop by that name established the principles of the Greek Orthodox Church — Basil for years took on the aura of aquiline-nosed upper-class Britishness of Sherlock Holmes portrayer Basil Rathbone, then spiced with the fragrant aroma of the herb that entered with the pesto generation.

Now, it's time to take a fresh look at Basil.

Basil was on the U.S. popularity list quite regularly up till 1970, reaching a high of Number 328 in 1904. Its history includes several rulers of the Byzantine Empire and Eastern Orthodox saints, including one whose grandmother, father, older sister and two younger brothers were all saints as well.

Basil has also been seen as a figure of fun, as in the manic Basil Fawlty in the British TV comedy classic *Fawlty Towers*, in the Disney movie *Basil of Baker Street*, and as Basil Brush and Basil Wombat in other kids' entertainment.

The Russian version, Vassily, is another possibility.

Bastian

Diminutive of Sebastian, Latin from Greek, "man of Sebastia"

In Spanish cultures, and spelled either Bastian or Bastien, this is a fairly common nickname name. The German fantasy children's book *The Neverending Story* features a young boy character called Bastian Balthazar Bux, and it has also been seen in several screen versions.

Bastian has been enjoying recent popularity in Latin America: it reached Number 11 in Chile — as well as in Germany and Scandinavia, and is just beginning to be appreciated here. Jeremy Sisto used it for his son.

Alternate spelling Bastien is also a fashionable euro form with a possible future in America. There is a one-act comic opera by Mozart titled *Bastien und Bastienne*.

Baxter

English occupational name, "baker"

An "x" makes any name cooler, so that Baxter has a bit more pizzazz than the original Baker. Baxter had some currency as a first name a century ago — it was on the popularity lists sporadically from 1880 till the 1920s, peaking at Number 515 in 1886 — which means it's just about due for a comeback. And we can see Bax as a worthy follow-up to Max and Jax.

Singer Ian Dury named his now-grown son Baxter, and Dr. Baxter Stockman was a scientist in the *Teenage Mutant Ninja Turtle* series.

Baz

Diminutive of Sebastian, "man of Sebastia" or Basil, "regal"

As Bas, it's a popular name in The Netherlands, but Baz, as in director Luhrmann, has potential for independent life too.

Curiously, Australian-born *Moulin Rouge* and *The Great Gatsby* director Luhrmann was born neither Sebastian nor Basil, but had the name Mark Anthony on his birth certificate; his nickname arose from his supposed resemblance to a British TV fox puppet named Basil Brush.

Beau

French, "handsome"

Beau suggests someone devilishly handsome, with a large measure of southern charm — a nice image to bestow on your boy. Often solely a nickname in the past, it's now standing firmly on its own — this year ranking at Number 311. Beau has been on the Social Security list non-stop since 1967, reaching a high of Number 203 in 1980.

Beau also has something of a dapper image, thanks to the fashionable Beau Brummell (born George), which led to the stylish New York mayor Jimmy Walker being called Beau James. Other notable Beaus had more formal names at birth — Beaus Bridges and Biden were both the third sons in their families to carry their fathers' names — Lloyd Vernet Bridges III and Joseph Robinette Biden III.

The novel *Beau Geste* was a major bestseller in its day and was also a popular movie — in that case Michael was the character's birth name, and many will remember that the child of Ashley and Melanie Wilkes in *Gone With the Wind* was called Beau, and there was also a Beau on the old TV western Maverick.

And if you want a more substantial name on the birth certificate, try Beauregard.

Art Garfunkel, Emma Bunton, Jamie-Lynn Sigler and Wendy Wilson all have sons named Beau.

Becan

Irish, "little man"

This more user-friendly Anglicized form of Beacan, could profit from its kinship with the popular Beckett — with which it could share the nickname Beck. Becan is an Irish saint's name, attached to the founder of a sixth-century monastery.

For ease of pronunciation, it can also be spelled Beccan.

Beckett

English and Irish, "bee hive, little brook or bee cottage"

Beckett is one of the big baby name hits of the decade.

A handsome name with an attractively brisk sound, and rich in literary associations via major Irish playwright Samuel Beckett, it is especially hot among celebs. Melissa Etheridge jump-started the trend in 1998, followed by Conan O'Brien, Stella McCartney, Malcolm McDowell, Nicole Sullivan and Natalie Maines. In the past year alone, Beckett's popularity has shot up 16 places to Number 314, after only appearing for the first time in 2006!

Another worthy namesake is the martyred saint Thomas à Becket, Archbishop of Canterbury, whose story was the basis of the Anouilh play *Becket*, which became a film starring Richard Burton and Peter O'Toole.

In 2005, the authors of *Freakonomics* predicted that Beckett would be one of the most popular names of 2015. They could be right!

Benedict

Latin, "blessed"

Parents who like Ben and Benjamin but find those forms too popular sometimes consider Benedict as a more distinctive choice. Unlike the Old Testament Benjamin, Benedict is the name of the saint who formed the Benedictine Order and of fifteen popes, including a recent one.

Shakespeare used a variant form — Benedick — for the character in *Much Ado About Nothing*. Other options are Bennett and Benno.

Benedict Cumberbatch is a rising British stage, film and TV actor, who has been seen as Stephen Hawking, William Pitt, Dr. Frankenstein, Frankenstein's monster, and recently as Sherlock Holmes in the BBC series.

Just one caveat: There is the link to that infamous traitor, Benedict Arnold.

Benjamin

Hebrew, "son of the right hand"

Benjamin is a biblical name that has enjoyed widespread favor for decades — and is attractive and strong enough to have entered the Top 20. One of those golden boys' names that feels traditional as well as sensitive and stylish, Benjamin has the further advantage of the friendly, accessible nickname Ben.

In the Old Testament, Benjamin was the youngest of the twelve sons of Jacob and Rachel in the Book of Genesis, and one of the founders of the twelve tribes of Israel. There have been numerous other notable Benjamin namesakes that followed, from Benjamin Franklin to Dr. Benjamin Spock. The name's popularity spiked after the release of *The Graduate* in 1967, with Dustin Hoffman playing the iconic Benjamin Braddock. Two recent, high-profile baby Benjamins were born to Kelly Preston and John Travolta, and to Gisele Bündchen and Tom Brady.

Bennett

English, medieval form of Benedict, "blessed"

Bennett is Ben with a bow tie, kind of a cross between Benjamin and Beckett. And it's one of the fastest-rising boy names, jumping from Number 362 to Number 202 in the last four years alone — and its choice by *30 Rock*'s Jane Krakowski could shoot it even higher.

Bennett Cerf was an eminent publisher — one of the founders of Random House — and renowned punster.

Bennett is a Top 75 surname, and has many noteworthy bearers, from Jane Austen's *Pride and Prejudice* family to indomitable singer Tony.

Benno

German, "bear"

Benno is a cool name in its own right — there was a tenth-century Saint Benno — though it is also used as a lively nickname for Benjamin. Saint Benno of Meissen is the patron saint of anglers and weavers and, strangely enough, alliteration.

Benno came to attention in the U.S. via the father and son duo of Benno Schmidt Sr and Jr Senior was the venture capitalist who invented the term venture capitalist and Junior was the president of Yale University. Benno is also the appellation of a student character in Umberto Eco's *The Name of the Rose*.

Bing

German, "kettle-shaped hollow"

When Kate Hudson named her second son Bingham and announced that she would be calling him Bing, it put this zingy nickname name out on the table. Before that, there was only one, further nicknamed Der Bingle — and he was really Harry Lillis Crosby.

And nowadays it's also a Microsoft search engine — but in any case, Bing has a lot of zing.

Birch

Tree name

Birch is a rarely used nature name that calls to mind the lovely image of the tall, strong but graceful white-barked tree.

The best known bearer of the name is former high-ranking Democratic Senator Birch Evans Bayh, who carried the name of his father and was the principal Senate sponsor of the Equal Rights Amendment.

The birch tree has many notable qualities and uses — including the making of furniture, paper, canoes, and drums, is considered the national tree of Russia (where it used to be worshiped as a goddess), the state tree of New Hampshire, and has spiritual significance in several cultures.

Bix

Modern nickname

Bix is a cool and jazzy nickname name, thanks to that final "x." It's largely associated with the legendary and influential cornet player (and inspiration for the novel *Young Man With a Horn*), Bix Beiderbecke. He was born Leon Bismark Beiderbecke and his nickname derived from his middle name.

Bix could easily fit in with cousins Jax, Dax, etc.

Bjorn

Swedish, "bear"

Bjorn is one of the most recognizable Scandinavian names, thanks in large part to tennis great Björn Borg, winner of five consecutive Wimbledon singles titles and six French opens and something of a rock star figure.

Bjorn has been in use since the days of the Vikings, but got a boost in popularity when Borg ruled the courts. There have also been other notable Bjorns in various fields in Sweden, Norway and Germany, ranging from the first king of Norway to a member of the pop group ABBA.

And if you do pick this name for your son, your baby Bjorn can be carried around in a Baby Bjorn.

Blaise

French, "to lisp, stammer"

As modern as it sounds, Blaise is an ancient Christian martyr name, and also in Arthurian legend the name of Merlin the Magician's secretary. Its relation to the word and name Blaze gives it a fiery feel. Amanda Beard named her baby boy Blaise Ray.

Saint Blaise, an Armenian bishop, is the patron saint of wild animals and those with sore throats. Blaise Pascal was the seventeenth-century French mathematician-physicist-inventor-writer-philosopher among whose many accomplishments was the invention of the calculator. And in the modern world, Blaise Zambini is a minor character in the *Harry Potter* franchise.

Blaise has been on the lower rungs of the popularity ladder since 1996, while Blaze ranks somewhat higher.

Boaz

Hebrew, "swiftness"

Now that such Old Testament patriarchs as Elijah and Moses fill the playground, Boaz seems downright baby-friendly, having more pizzazz than many of the others, perhaps as a successor to Noah. A name that was used by the seventeenth-century Pilgrims and is still heard in Israel, but is a rarity in the U.S., Boaz is associated with the Jewish holiday Shavuot, as that is when the Bible story of Ruth is read in the synagogue, and Boaz was Ruth's wealthy and generous second husband, making it logical for Boaz to sometimes be given to boys born at that time.

Extra added attraction: one of the all-time great nicknames — Bo.

Bodhi

Sanskrit, "awakening, enlightenment"

A surprise success in the baby name world, Bodhi is a Sanskrit name translated as "enlightenment" or "awakening," which relates to a Buddhist concept, wherein Bodhi is synonymous with the state of nirvana, being freed from hate, greed and ego. The Bodhi tree is a large fig tree under which the founder of Buddhism received enlightenment.

Bodhi has recently been appearing as a baby name in the American celebrisphere, first heard via Bodhi Elfman, husband of Jenna. Since then it has been used by Amy Brenneman and Oliver Hudson for their sons, and by celebrity chef Tom Colicchio as the middle name for his boy, Luka. Carly Simon and James Taylor have a grandson named Bodhi. And who remembers that it was the name of the Patrick Swayze character in the 1991 film *Point Break*?

As opposed to some other religious and spiritual names, Bodhi has an upbeat, friendly feel, similar to that of Brody and Cody.

Booker

English occupational surname, "scribe"
Booker would make for a very cool name for writers, reformers, R & B fans and those wanting to pay tribute to Booker T. Washington.

T. (for Thomas) Boone Pickens is a high-profile business magnate; Boone Carlyle was a fiery character on TV's *Lost*.

Boris

Slavic, "to fight"
Boris is one of the old Russian names being revived by chic Europeans; it hasn't quite made a comeback yet in the U.S., but it does have potential.

For a long time the name has been associated with Boris Karloff, famed for playing Frankenstein's monster; he was William Henry Pratt before taking on the more exotic stage name of Boris — and the Karloff fear factor may have kept some parents away.

A Russian saint's name, Boris has other more benign and inspiring namesakes like German-born tennis champ Boris Becker and writer Boris Pasternak, author of *Dr. Zhivago*, as well as the early Russian Tsar Boris Gudonov, son-in-law of Ivan the Terrible, the subject of the Mussorgsky opera.

Boris Trigorin is a main character in the Chekhov play *The Seagull*.

Bowen

Welsh, "son of Owen"
Bowen is a Celtic surname representing two separate Celtic strains, one Welsh and one Irish, and entered the Top 1000 for the first time in 2011.

Football Hall of Famer Drew Brees named his son Bowen, as did a recent reality show couple looking for the perfect name to "brand" their baby. It does have the appealing nickname Bo.

Bowen could be a fresher alternative to Owen or Rowan.

Bowie

Scottish, "blond"

Baseball commissioner Bowie Kuhn put this name in play as a first name, but David Bowie (born with the considerably less marketable moniker of David Robert Jones) dyed it blond and gave it charisma. He changed his surname in 1965 to avoid confusion with the then popular Davy Jones of The Monkees. The name Bowie reputedly came about as a reference to the American hero of the Alamo, Jim Bowie.

Bowie successfully combines all these positive elements — Gaelic charm, a Western drawl and musical cred.

Brady

Irish, "broad meadow," "large-chested"

The name given to Miranda Hobbes's son on the dearly departed *Sex and the City* is a friendly and energetic choice. You well might want to make your son part of the Brady bunch.

Brady has been a well-used boy's name since the turn-of-the-last-century Diamond Jim Brady days, but it's had its highest numbers in the past two decades, now slightly down at Number 136.

Brady Fuller is a young werewolf in the *Twilight* series, but there were more notable Bradys bearing it as a surname, including Civil War photographer Mathew, press secretary James, and quarterback Tom — in addition of course to Mike, Carol, Greg, Marsha, and Jan et al.

Bram

Dutch variation of Abraham, Hebrew, "father of multitudes"

Bram has an unusual measure of character and charm for a one-syllable name; it started as a hipper-than-Abe diminutive of the biblical Abraham, but is also an independent Irish and Dutch name, made famous by Irish-born *Dracula* creator Bram (nee Abraham) Stoker. Bram is currently Number 16 in the Netherlands; Bram Howard was a character on *The West Wing*.

Another route to Bram is Bramwell, as in early actor Bramwell Fletcher, who — speaking of horror movies — was noted for his mad scenes in the 1932 film *The Mummy*.

Branch

Word name

Branch is an attractive name with associations both with trees and with branching out into brave new worlds. Baseball's Branch (born Wesley, with Branch as his middle name)

Rickey broke the color barrier by hiring Jackie Robinson for the Dodgers. Like Leaf, Branch makes a nice, not-so-obvious, addition to the tree category.

Brennan

Irish, "descendent of the sad one"

Brennan is a winning Irish surname name, more modern than Brian or Brendan, more unusual than Conor and Aidan. The only possible problem with Brennan: people might think you're saying Brendan.

Brennan eased onto the very bottom of the popularity list in 1966, and has pretty much remained ever since, now at Number 318.

Brice

Scottish surname, "speckled, freckled"

Brice, often spelled Bryce, is an old saint's name that now has a sleek and sophisticated image — it feels elegant and efficient. Of the two spellings, Bryce is now the more popular, though either would make a nice update for a Grandpa Bruce.

Ron Howard did a bit of gender bending when he called his daughter Bryce Dallas — a name now featured on marquees. Painter Brice Marden represents the other spelling, while St. Brice was a fifth-century Frenchman who was a disciple and successor of St. Martin as bishop of Tours.

Brock

English, "badger"

Brock is a rock solid name, with a touch of preppy sophistication. It has ranked solidly in the Top 400 since 1975.

Among Brocks who lived up to their name are Brock Peters (actually born George), who played Tom Robinson in *To Kill a Mockingbird*, Brock Pemberton, a founder of the Tony Awards, and Brock Chisholm, the first Director-General of the World Health Organization.

Brock is the traditional name given to a badger in folk tales.

Brody

Irish, "ditch"

The energetic Brody is a perfect example of when bad meanings happen to good names. Brody is slightly less common than Brady, making it a more distinctive choice — even though Brody has been in the Top 100 for the past five years, now at Number 91.

Bruce Jenner named his son Brody before he fell under the sway of the Kardashian K-naming klan.

Brogan

Irish, possibly "small shoe"

Brogan is a cheerful Irish surname that would fit right in with the Logans and "Br"-starting names now trendy for boys. It's been on the pop list for the past three years, though it's sliding again. Its history includes Saint Brogan (Broccan in Gaelic), who was Saint Patrick's nephew and scribe.

In *Shrek Forever After* Brogan was an ogre voiced by Jon Hamm. Supposedly, the character was almost called Gnimrahc — or Charming spelled backwards. Brogan is better.

Bronson

English, "son of brown-haired one"

This neglected surname has a modern yet old New England feel, perhaps because of the association with the transcendental teacher and reformer Bronson (born Amos Bronson) Alcott, father of Louisa May. (One-time sitcom star Bronson Pinchot's full name is Bronson Alcott Pinchot.) A more muscular image comes via tough guy Charles Bronson.

Brown

Color and surname

Most color names, like Scarlet and Violet, are definitely female, but not this one. Brown is as rich and warm as the tone it denotes, though we must admit the Italian version Bruno has more spark and substance.

Bruno

German, "brown"

Bruno is a popular name throughout Europe and South America that deserves more fashion status here. Stylish British cookbook writer Nigella Lawson has a son named Bruno. The versatile singer-songwriter Bruno Mars, who was raised in Hawaii, was originally named Peter, but was given the nickname Bruno at the age of two. Another Bruno: *Dancing With the Stars* judge Bruno Tonioli.

St. Bruno of Cologne was a nobleman who founded the Carthusian order of monks in 1084. Bruno is a name often used for bears in children's stories, and Lewis Carroll wrote one called *Sylvie and Bruno*. More recently, Bruno is the central character in Irish Murdoch's novel, *Bruno's Dream*.

A reference to ignore: the Sacha Baron Cohen character in "Bruno."

Burl

English, "knotty wood," "butler"

This name has a nicely fragrant woodsy feel, bringing it into the nature-tree name category. Its only well-known bearer, folk singer and Oscar-winning actor Burl Ives, had the full birth certificate name of Burl Icle Ivanhoe Ives — nothing compared to his two siblings named Argola and Lillburn.

Byron

English, "barn for cows"

For centuries, this name had a romantic, windswept image due to its strong connection to the poet Lord Byron, who inspired its use as a first name. It is one of those surprise names that's appeared on the Top 1000 every year since 1880, though now is at its nadir at Number 540.

William Faulkner used Byron for characters in two of his novels — *Light in August* and *The Town*. It was seen as a character on *Arrested Development* (the real name of Buster), is the appellation of several high-scoring athletes, was given to his son by *Lost*'s Matthew Fox in 2001 and — trivia tidbit bonus — was James Dean's middle name.

C

Cade

English, "round" or "barrel"

Strong, ultramasculine, and modern, Cade shot up the popularity lists — it's been as high as Number 201 — along with cousins Caden and Cale. Like Scarlett, Rhett, Ashley, Melanie and Beau, it was worn by a character in *Gone With the Wind.*

There's a Cade Skywalker in the *Star Wars* universe, and Keith Carradine named his now grown son Cade.

Cagney

Irish, "tribute"

Cagney is one of the spunkiest Irish surnames around, and could make a lively and fresher successor to the tired Casey.

James Cagney will be remembered not only for his iconic gangster films, but also for his Academy-Award-winning performance as song-and-dance man George M. Cohan in *Yankee Doodle Dandy. Cagney & Lacey* was a popular 1980s police drama.

Caleb

Hebrew, "devotion to God"

Caleb is an attractive Old Testament name, one that is now following in hot pursuit of Jacob as a leading biblical boy's name. It has been in the Top 40 since 2000, now ranking at Number 32.

In the Old Testament, Caleb is one of only two ancient Israelites (Joshua was the other) who set out from Egypt to finally enter the promised land.

Julianne Moore chose Caleb for her son, as did Bo Bice. The short form Cale is also rising in popularity, and the current Kaleb spelling picks up on the "C-to-K" initial trend.

Caleb Garth is a character in George Eliot's *Middlemarch*. Caleb was the full name of James Dean's character Cal in *East of Eden,* and the name has also been heard on *Desperate Housewives* and *Buffy the Vampire Slayer.*

Calixto

Greek, "beautiful"

Calixto is known in Spain as the name of three popes, one of whom was the martyr, Callixtus I, regarded as a saint. Calixto has a lot of energy and futuristic spirit, thanks in part to the attention-grabbing "x." He is the main character in the Spanish classic, Fernando de Rojas's *Tragicomedy of Calisto and Melibea*.

Calloway

Irish from Latin, "pebbly place"

Calloway is one of those irresistibly jaunty, animated three-syllable Irish surnames, like Sullivan and Finnegan — but this one has the added attraction of jazzy ties to the immortal "Dean of American Jive," Cab Calloway.

There was a 1951 comedy spoof called *Calloway Went Thataway*.

Callum

Scottish from Latin, Columba, "dove"

Callum, a charming Scottish boys' name just beginning to be heard in this country but high on the list in England, Scotland and Northern Ireland, is worth consideration as a less popular alternative to Colin and Caleb, etc.

Kyle MacLachlan chose Callum for his son. Callum might also be spelled Calum; in Ireland, the name became Colm, and in Scotland it's sometimes used as a pet form of Malcolm.

Callum was popular among early Christians because the dove was a symbol of purity, peace and the Holy Spirit. St. Columba was one of the most influential of the early Celtic saints.

Calvin

Latin, "bald, hairless"

Calvin is a slightly quirky but cozy name that has a fashion edge thanks to Calvin Klein. It has been steadily on the popularity list since records were kept, never lower than Number 250, peaking in the 1920s, the era of the Calvin (originally John Calvin) Coolidge presidency.

The name came into use as a first name in honor of John Calvin — born Jehan Cauvin — the seventeenth-century French Protestant reformer whose strict doctrines became the basis of Calvinism, and the name was taken up as a tribute to him.

Other associations include the above-mentioned Calvin Klein (and his famous "Calvins" ads), humorous writer Calvin Trillin, the comic strip "Calvin & Hobbes" — and it's also the birth name of Snoop Dog.

Canyon

Spanish word name

Canyon is a quasi-unique name evocative of natural splendor and the old Steve Canyon comic-strip heroism, making it an intriguing new word-name possibility.

Similar but less word-like: Kenyon.

Carson

Irish and Scottish, "son of the marsh-dwellers"

Carson is an androgynous executive-type name, with a dash of the Wild West via the legendary Missouri frontiersman Kit Carson. Dating back to when it was the name of Nancy Drew's Dad, Carson is still steadily in the Top 100, reaching its highest point at Number 80 in 2010.

Current Carsons include TV personalities Carson Daly and Carson Kressley, and Heisman Trophy-winning quarterback Carson Palmer. Carson Wells was the bounty hunter character played by Woody Harrelson in *No Country for Old Men*, and Carson is the name chosen by actress Kathryn Erbe for her son.

Although its best known namesake is writer Carson McCullers, Carson has not caught on as a girl's name.

Carter

English occupational name, "transporter of goods by cart"

Carter has been popular for almost two decades, but only now has it broken into the Top 40, leaving all the other upscale occupational surname names behind. Having hot characters named Carter on both *Gossip Girl* and *The OC* probably didn't hurt, and for fifteen years on *ER*, Noah Wyle's Dr. John Carter was always called by his last name. Carter also, of course, has presidential cred.

While Carter sits at Number 36 across the country, it is especially loved in the Midwest, having been Number 2 in Nebraska and Number 3 in Iowa, as well as spreading north to Saskatchewan (Number 2) and Manitoba (Number 5).

Carver

English, "wood carver"

Carver is an occupational name with an artistic bent, as is the newly arrived Painter, which has a fresher feel than the 1990s Carter. It also has eminent last-name links to botanist and educator George Washington Carver and short story master Raymond Carver.

Carver appears as a character in the R. D. Blackmore classic *Lorna Doone*.

Casper

Dutch form of Jasper, Persian, "treasurer"
This ancient name, also spelled Caspar, is finally shedding its ghostly image and moving into the twenty-first century. Popular in the Netherlands and Scandinavia, where it's sometimes shorted to Cas, Casper could ride the style coattails of cousin Jasper. Casper was one of the Three Magi who brought gifts to the infant Jesus along with Melchior and Balthasar.

Some notable Caspers are one-time Secretary of Defense Caspar Weinberger (called Cap) and actor Casper Van Dien, whose son is Casper Robert Van Dien III. Claudia Schiffer and Jenny Frost both used the names for their boys, while Jason Lee did a gender switch when he called his daughter Casper (sister of Pilot Inspektor).

Casper Goodwood was the persistent suitor of the main character, Isabel Archer, in Henry James's novel *A Portrait of a Lady*.

Caspian

Place name
One of the most romantic of appellations, as well as being a geographical name of the large salty sea between Asia and Europe that probably inspired C.S. Lewis to use it for the name of the hero of his children's novel, *Prince Caspian*, part of the *Chronicles of Narnia* series.

Caspian is attracting a lot of attention from cutting-edge parents these days.

Cassian

English variation of Cassius, Latin, "hollow"
Cassian is a saints' and Latin clan name, related to Cassius, that is virtually unused and waiting to be discovered.

There have been at least four fourth- and fifth-century St. Cassians, one of whom is the patron saint of (not many of them left) stenographers. John Cassian was a monk and ascetic writer who introduced Eastern monasticism into the West.

Patrick Wilson used the alternate spelling Kassian for his son.

Cassius

Latin, "hollow"
Cassius is a Shakespearean name with the feel of antiquity that is coming into fashion. Cassius Clay was an abolitionist, and the birth name of Muhammad Ali. It was chosen for their sons by singer Bobby Brown and Getty heir/actor Balthazar Getty. Vanessa Marcil and Brian Austin Green used the nouveau Kassius spelling for theirs.

Cassius is one of a number of "Cas"-starting names drawing attention, including Caspian, Cassian, Castor, Casper, Cashel, and Cash. Cass and Cash are both accessible nicknames

Cato

Latin, "all-knowing"

Cato conjures up images of ancient Roman statesmen and southern antebellum retainers; it could have revival potential, with its "O" ending and the current interest in the names of Greek and Roman antiquity.

The Roman statesman known as Cato the Elder was born Marcus Portius, the Cato added in tribute to his natural sagacity, practical wisdom and political expertise.

Cato appears in Shakespeare's *Julius Caesar* and, to go from the sublime to the ridiculous, in the *Pink Panther* movies — and Kato was The Green Hornet's valet. Cato is also a twenty-first-century *Hunger Games* name, which could do more to spur its popularity than all its past history.

Cedar

English, tree name

Cedar is, like Ash, Oak, Pine and Ebony, one of the new tree/wood names that parents are starting to consider; this one is particularly aromatic.

In the Bible the cedar is mentioned in Psalm 92:12: "The righteous shall flourish like the palm tree and grow like a cedar in Lebanon." The Lebanon Cedar was used to build King Solomon's temple in Jerusalem, and there are now several hospitals called Cedars of Lebanon, plus a U2 song by that name.

A contemporary bearer of the name was the jazz pianist Cedar Walton.

Cedric

Celtic, "bounty"

Cedric was invented by Sir Walter Scott for the noble character of the hero's father in *Ivanhoe*, presumed to be an altered form of the Saxon name Cerdic. The name then lost some testosterone as Little Lord Fauntleroy, the long-haired, velvet-suited and lace-collared boy hero of the Frances Hodgson Burnett book, who became an unwitting symbol of the pampered mama's boy.

Since then that stereotype has been broken principally by the handsome *Harry Potter* character Cedric Diggory, played by the teen-aged pre-*Twilight* Robert Pattinson, and it, like cousin Cecil, is at the point of being rediscovered by cutting-edge namers.

Charles

French from German, "free man"

Charles is a longtime traditional favorite that was in the Top 10 until the 1960s. Lately Charles has been resuscitated by many celeb parents, from Jodie Foster to Russell Crowe, honoring a distinguished history dating back to the emperor Charlemagne — the original Charles the Great.

Charles has been so well used for so long that it is virtually faceless — it can conjure up anyone from Dickens to Chaplin to Bronson. It has been an elegant royal name — designating both Bonnie Prince Charlie, leader of a 1745 rebellion, and the present Prince of Wales, as well as kings of France, Spain, England, Portugal and Hungary.

Nickname Charlie (and Charley) has taken on a life of its own and is now a popular choice for both sexes. And though Chuck is now virtually gone, Chaz/Chazz is becoming a nickname of choice.

Among the well-used international versions of Charles: Carl, Carlo, Carlos, Karel, Xarles, Charlot and Siarl.

Charlie

English, diminutive of Charles, "free man"

Charlie is one of the friendliest names on the planet, and Good-time Charlie is back. More and more parents (of babies of both genders) these days are opting to put the friendly, genial Charlie on birth certificates — though we'd recommend you use Charlie as a pet form of the more serious Charles. In the U.K., Charlie is the fourth most popular name for boys.

Charlie has dozens and dozens of pop cultural references, from Charlie Chaplin to Charlie McCarthy to *Charlie's Angels* to Charlie Parker to Charlie Sheen to Charlie Rose. It derives, of course, from the classic name Charles which, in turn, comes from a German word meaning "free man." Charles became very popular in France during the Middle Ages due to the fame of Charles the Great, aka Charlemagne.

Putting nicknames on the birth certificate is very much a growing trend. Current celebs who have chosen Charlie for their sons include Tiger Woods, Mimi Rogers, Soledad O'Brien and Sarah Chalke.

Chase

French, "to hunt"

Chase, with its sleek and ultra-prosperous aura, is redolent of the worlds of high finance and international banking. Chase has been well used during the last decade, seen as a character on *24* and on several young-audience shows. Chase is mega-popular in some parts of Canada — it was recently as high as Number 9 in Saskatchewan.

There are a disproportionate number of football stars name Chase.

Variation Chace began catching on in 2008, thanks largely to *Gossip Girl* hottie Chace (born Christopher Chace) Crawford.

Cheever

English, "female goat"

Cheever has a nice, cheery sound, literary ties to novelist and short writer John Cheever and to the Edwin Arlington Robinson narrative poem *Miniver Cheevy*, as well as a subliminal association with the desirable word achiever: all strong pluses.

Chester

Latin, "fortress, walled town," place name

Chester is a comfortable, little-used teddy-bear of a name that suddenly sounds both quirky and cuddly.

Chester was a Top 100 name from the 1880s to 1929, gradually fading till it finally dropped off the list completely in 1995. It's been seen on old TV shows like *Gunsmoke* and *The Life of Riley*, then reappeared later on *The Nanny* and *The Wire*. Chester Alan Arthur made it presidential, it was a World War II hero via Admiral Chester Nimitz, the comic world associates it with Chester Gould, creator of Dick Tracy, and it has modern musical ties to Chester Bennington, lead singer of Linkin Park.

Tom Hanks and Rita Wilson have a son named Chester.

Nickname Chet has, like Hank, a friendly retro vibe.

Christo

Slavic, "one who carries Christ"

This unusual name, which is jauntier than Chris when used as a diminutive of Christopher, is associated with the Bulgarian installation artist of that name, responsible for wrapping many public institutions and known especially for *The Gates of Central Park* and *Running Fence*. Christo is his full given name.

Clancy

Irish, "red-haired warrior"

Clancy, one of the original crossover Irish surname names, is as energetic and appealing as ever — full of moxie, more distinctive than Casey, and also one of the less obvious of the red-headed names.

A literary namesake is Clancy Sigal, author of the autobiographical novel *Going Away*, and there is also the comical mid-century song, *Clancy Lowered the Boom*.

More common as a last name than a first, Clancy has gained fame via the Irish folk music group the Clancy Brothers, and one of the bestselling authors of all time, Tom Clancy, known for his espionage and techno thrillers.

Clark

English, "scribe, secretary, cleric, scholar, clerk"
Clark seemed to have been Gone with the Wind, but parents looking for a short, strong boy's name are now beginning to appreciate its cool combination of Gable charm with Superman power.

Clark, now ranking Number 554, has been steadily on the popularity list — it was 176 in 1881 and well used in the 1940s and 50s — and is now on another upswing.

Long-term Hollywood heartthrob Clark Gable was born William Clark — his middle name was the maiden name of his maternal grandmother.

Claude

French from Latin, "lame"
Claude is a soft-spoken French name that conjures up the pastel colors of Monet and harmonies of Debussy. In France, it is used for girls as well; in fact, in the Tracy Chevalier novel *Lady and the Unicorn*, the protagonist is a female Claude.

Claudes have appeared in such iconic movies as *Chinatown* and *Close Encounters of the Third Kind*. Actor Simon Baker has a son named Claude Blue.

A French classic, Claude was also a top 100 name in the US until 1922.

The attractive Italian version Claudio is occasionally heard in this country and Claudius is the original Latin — which could be restored in the current Latin-loving climate.

Clay

English word name; diminutive of Clayton
Clay is a rich, earthy one-syllable name with a southern-inflected handsome-rogue image, featured on soap operas and reality TV, whose numbers have dropped over the past few years, but could make a comeback. Its longer forms are Clayton and Clayborne.

There have been TV characters called Clay on *The Wire* and *Sons of Anarchy*, and the name's most prominent recent bearers are American Idol Clay (born Clayton) Aiken and Green Bay Packer linebacker Clay (born William Clay) Matthews.

Clement

Latin, "mild, merciful"

Clement, the name of fourteen popes and several saints, has a pleasantly positive, slightly antiquated feel, like the phrase "clement weather."

Clement C. Moore wrote the poem *A Visit from St. Nicholas*, Clement Attlee was a prominent post-World War II British Prime Minister, and Clement Greenberg was the art critic who promoted Abstract Expressionism.

The hero of Thomas Hardy's *The Return of the Native* is Clement Yeobright, known as Clym rather than the usual Clem.

Clive

English, "lives near a high cliff"

Clive used to be stereotyped as a clipped British name in a pith helmet and pencil-thin moustache, as in English military hero Clive of India — but this image has been turned on its ear by hunky Clive Owen.

William Makepeace Thackeray did a lot to launch this as a first name via his novel *The Newcomes* with Clive Newcombe being the hero — most likely inspired by the exploits of General Robert Clive, essentially the founder of British India.

Two other notable modern day Clives are writers Barker and Cussler.

Clyde

Scottish river name

Even though in the past Clyde may have been identified as half of the infamous outlaw duo with partner Bonnie Parker — especially after the 1967 movie in which he was played by Warren Beatty — Clyde has always had an element of jazzy cool that could overcome all the rest. The name relates to the River Clyde that runs through the city of Glasgow. It was a Top 100 name in the US through the 1930s.

Clyde Griffiths was the doomed protagonist of Theodore Dreiser's novel *An American Tragedy* — though his name was changed to George in the film. In the field of sports, basketball Hall of Famer — and later *Dancing with the Stars* participant — Clyde Drexler was known as Clyde the Slide, and Walt Frazier's nickname was Clyde. Catherine Keener and Dermot Mulroney have a son named Clyde.

Cole

English, "swarthy, coal black"; also diminutive of Nicholas

Cole — a short name that embodies a lot of richness and depth — has long been associated with the great songwriter Cole Porter. Currently, Cole, which has been on a roll since the mid-90s, is holding on to its steady popularity, now at Number 102. It's also a Top 50 name in Scotland.

Old King Cole — which refers to a real British king — is familiar to all kids. Cole was the name of the child in *The Sixth Sense* and was also the name of — sorry — the notorious outlaw Cole Younger, who was born Thomas Coleman.

Colt

Word name
Colt is the kind of unconventionally macho name that is so trendy right now, because of or despite its association with horses and guns. Colt rose about a whopping 200 places in popularity over the last four years to Number 328!

Samuel Colt was the inventor and industrialist credited with popularizing the revolver.

Colt is a perfect jock name, associated both with Cleveland Browns quarterback Colt McCoy and an entire football team.

Colton

English, "from the coal or dark town"
Colton is a trendy two-syllable choice, with the popular "on/en" ending.

Colton jumped onto the popularity list in 1982 at Number 806. Then, in 1988, the hunky character Colton Shore was introduced on the soap opera *General Hospital*, and the name began to zoom up the list, till it has now reached Number 65. Coincidence or contributing factor?

Another attractive namesake is *Teen Wolf* heartthrob Colton Haynes.

Conan

Irish, "little wolf"
The fierce image of the Barbarian made a complete turnaround thanks to amiable talk show host O'Brien, making Conan one of the newly desirable Irish choices, a perfect alternative to Conor/Connor.

In Gaelic, Conan was the name of an illustrious seventh-century Irish saint, bishop of the Isle of Man. Sherlock Holmes creator Arthur Conan Doyle was born in Scotland, of Irish stock.

Connor

Irish, "lover of hounds"
Connor, the appealing name of an early semi-legendary king of Ulster in Irish mythology, is now just inside the Top 60 — taken together with its alternate Conor

spelling would bring it even higher on the list — while in its native Ireland the Conor version is the fifth most popular boys' name.

Connor MacLeod was the name of the title character in the 1986 film *The Highlander*, which helped promote the name.

Nicole Kidman and Tom Cruise have a teen-aged son named Connor, while Eric Clapton has a younger Conor; the name of the Irish writer and historian is spelled Conor Cruise O'Brien.

Since Connor means "lover of hounds," it might make a good choice for a dog-loving family. In fact, one of the sons in *Marley and Me* is given that name.

Conrad

German, "brave counsel"

Conrad has a somewhat intellectual masculine image, a solid name that has been consistently on the popularity lists, especially well used in the 1920s and 30s, and given a pop of rock energy by the Elvis-like character of Conrad Birdie in *Bye, Bye, Birdie* — ("We love you Conrad, oh yes we do!").

Conrad has been both a saints' name and a German royal appellation. One of its most well-known bearers is hotelier Conrad Hilton, great-grandfather of the Paris generation. Conrad was the prototypical Byronic hero of his poem *The Corsair*. There have been fictive Conrads on shows like *Weeds* and *CSI*.

Corrado is the attractive Italian form.

Constantine

Latin, "steadfast"

This Roman Emperor's name has long considered too grand for an American boy. But in this era of children named Augustine and Atticus, it just may be prime for an unlikely comeback.

Constantine the Great was the first Roman Emperor to convert to Christianity and issued the Edict of Milan, which proclaimed religious tolerance throughout the empire. Constantine was also the name of three medieval Scottish kings.

A modern bearer is Constantine Maroulis, singer and actor and *American Idol* finalist. The 2005 horror film *Constantine* featured a hero by that surname.

Advice: Find a nickname other than Connie or Con.

Cooper

English occupational name, "barrel maker"
The genial yet upscale and preppy Cooper was one of the first occupational last names to catch on — and Cooper remains a pleasing option.

Cooper began his rapid climb in 1982 and has been in the Top 1200 since 2007, now at Number 83. It is wildly popular in Australia, where in some areas Cooper is the top name.

Two surnamed Coopers currently shining a spotlight on the name: Anderson and Bradley, and Cooper/Coop is one of the doctors on *Nurse Jackie*.

Corbin

Latin, "crow"
Corbin, the name of the castle where the Holy Grail was said to be hidden, came to the fore in the 1980s via actor Corbin Bernsen when he was the high profile star of *LA Law*, but its use is only now escalating as part of the mania for two-syllable names starting with "c" or "k," as well as from the more youthful image of Corbin Bleu, the attractive actor-model-dancer-singer who was one of the stars of the Disney hit *High School Musical*.

Bruce Willis's character name in *The Fifth Element* was spelled Korben Dallas.

Cormac

Irish, "charioteer"
Both offbeat and upbeat, this evocative traditional Irish name that runs through Celtic mythology is known here via award-winning novelist Cormac McCarthy (born Charles). The author's adopted name is related to Cormac Mac Airt, one of the great legendary high kings of Ireland.

In two of the *Harry Potter* movies, Cormac McLaggen is a Gryffindor student.

And for all you popularity-phobes, Cormac has never yet made it onto the American Top 1000 list.

Cornelius

Latin, "horn"
Cornelius, the New Testament name of a third-century Pope and saint, is one of those venerable Latin names on the edge of consideration, despite the corny nickname alert.

Cornelius has some magical vibe via Cornelius Agrippa, a medieval alchemist who appears in scores of books, including *Frankenstein* and *Harry Potter*. In Christopher Marlowe's *Dr. Faustus*, Cornelius was one of the two magicians who help Faustus strike his bargain with the devil. Two characters of the name appear in Shakespeare's plays — *Hamlet* and *Cymbeline*. The most famous bearer of the name is probably railroad magnate Cornelius Vanderbilt, who gave the name an aristocratic air. Cornelius is also the birth name of Chevy Chase.

Cornelius was consistently in the Top 1000 until five years ago; it was a Top 300 name through 1933.

And if you're put off by the short form Corny, you could consider Neely, the nickname of the young Cornelius in *A Tree Grows in Brooklyn*.

Cosimo

Italian variation of Cosmo, "universe"

Dramatic, worldly, and exotic, Cosimo was chosen by singer Beck and his wife, Marissa Ribisi, for their son. Now that Cosima has emerged as a starbaby favorite, twin brother Cosimo could join her.

Cosimo de Medici was the first of the Medici dynasty to wield power in Florence during much of the Italian Renaissance, and was noted for his patronage of the arts. An inspirational name for creative parents.

Cosmo

Italian from Greek, "order, beauty"

We all heard it on *Seinfeld* as the long-concealed first name of Kramer, now some pioneering parents are wondering if this expansive Greek name that seems to embrace the whole cosmos could make a creative and cool choice for their baby.

Cosmo is the name of the Arabian-born patron saint of doctors.

In literature, Baron Cosmo Bradwardine is a character in Sir Walter Scott's novel *Waverly* and Cosmo Topper is the befuddled banker in Thorne Smith's humorous novel *Topper*.

In modern times Cosmo has become the short form for Cosmopolitan — both the magazine and the cocktail.

Crane

English surname, "crane"

This elegant surname has great potential to turn into an unusual first name, especially with its literary associations to both Stephen and Hart Crane.

Crane is a surname that originated for a tall man with long, thin legs. It can now be seen as one of the newly stylish bird names, like Wren and Lark, and could fit in well with future classmates Zane, Kane, Dane, Lane, Rain — and Jane.

Crispin

Latin, "curly-haired"

Crispin, which was introduced into the mainstream by actor Crispin Glover and which means "curly-haired" in Latin, has an image very much like its first syllable: crisp, autumnal, and colorful.

St. Crispin, the patron saint of shoemakers, died in the third century and, as rousingly referenced by Shakespeare, Henry V fought a great battle on St. Crispin's Day. Crispin Glover was actually named for the Shakespearean speech.

In the *Harry Potter* books, Crispin Cronk is an egyptophile wizard who kept several sphinxes in his backyard.

Crispian is an interesting, rarely used variation, as is Crispus, associated with African-American hero Crispus Atticus, the first colonist to die for independence in the Boston Massacre.

Crosby

Irish, "village with crosses"

Crosby is an attractively laid-back Irish surname with retro musical associations to Bing and Crosby, Stills, and Nash, and with a jaunty air. Crosby Braverman is currently the name of a character on the TV show *Parenthood*, played by Dax Shepard.

Crosby entered the Top 1000 list for the first time in 2011.

Cruz

Spanish, "cross"

For a single-syllable Latino surname, this new popular kid on the block packs a lot of energy and charm. Victoria and David Beckham named their third son Cruz, following Brooklyn and Romeo, and it was also picked up on by tennis star Lleyton Hewitt for his son. Other parents may prize its Christian associations.

Cruz is very much a unisex name in the Spanish culture, and is also a common surname, as in Penelope and Celia.

Cullen

Irish, "puppy, cub" or "handsome lad"

Cullen is an appealing Irish surname name that upped its cool factor considerably when it became the *Twilight* family name of Edward et al. It's also among the fastest rising boys' names, jumping a whopping 297 spots from 2008 to 2009, and then another 72 places in 2010 to become the 415th most popular choice in the country. In 2011, however, it dropped back down to 471.

Cullen Jenkins is a defensive tackle for the Philadelphia Eagles.

Curran

Irish surname from O Corrain, "descendant of Curran"

Curran is a common surname in Ireland, but unusual even there as a first. With its savory feel, calling to mind curry and currants, Curran can make for an attractive update on Colin or Connor.

Cyprian

Greek, "man of Cyprus"

With a long and noble history — Cyprian was one of the great Christian Latin writers — this could make a highly unusual but meaningful choice.

Cyprian has been in use since medieval times, initially made known via the third-century lawyer, martyr and bishop of Carthage, St. Cyprian, who wrote widely on theological themes.

There was a noted Nigerian writer named Cyprian Ekwensi, and a character named Cyprian in a Louise Erdrich novel, and in *Harry Potter*, Cyprian Youdle is a Quidditch referee.

Cyrus

Persian, "sun" or "throne"

Very popular in the Iranian community, this name of the founder of the Persian Empire has had a more down-home, corncob pipe-smoking image for most Americans in the past, but this has begun to change.

Cyrus McCormick was the inventor of the reaper; Cyrus Vance was Secretary of State under Jimmy Carter. The name is also associated these days with singer Miley Cyrus.

D

Dalton

English, "the settlement in the valley"

Dalton is a name with multi-faceted appeal. Many are attracted to the name's resemblance to other two-syllable "n" ending favorites: Colton, Holden, and cousins; others see it as a trendy Western name, recalling the legendary Dalton Brothers gang, and it also has something of an upscale, preppy feel connected to the exclusive New York private school. A Top 100 name in the 1990s, Dalton is still chosen by about 1,200 parents a year.

The most well-known bearer of the name is blacklisted screenwriter Dalton Trumbo, but there have been a number of high-profile fictional Daltons as well. Dalton Rumba is a current adult character on *Glee*, Clive Owen played a Dalton in *Inside Man*, there was a scholarly Dalton on *Buffy, the Vampire Slayer*, and Patrick Swayze opened the film *Roadhouse* by stating "My name is Dalton Russell."

Damian

Greek, "to tame, subdue"

Damian has sidestepped its demonic horror movie overtones, leaving a basically friendly and charming Irish image. A well-used upper-class name in England, it is growing in popularity here. It entered the ranks in 1952, has made a gradual climb to its current high point — Number 97.

There are several saints by this name, including an early one who was a renowned healer.

Damian Lewis is a British actor, the star of *Homeland*, Damian Marley, youngest son of Bob Marley, is a Grammy-winning reggae artist in his own right.

The French spelling Damien is also frequently used — it now ranks at Number 218.

Damon

English variation of Damian

Damon is a name with a strong, pleasing aura (much like the persona of Matt D.) and extremely positive ancient associations. From the classical myth, Damon and Pythias have become symbols of true friendship, as Damon risked his life to save his friend from execution. And Damon of Athens was the fifth-century philosopher who taught both Pericles and Socrates.

Other interesting associations: Damon Runyon wrote *Guys and Dolls*, Damon is one of the funny Wayans brothers, Damon Dash is a high profile music exec, and Damon Salvatore is a key figure in *The Vampire Diaries*.

Dane

English, "from Denmark" or variant of Dean

Dane is a more masculine Dana alternative, with added style edge. Dane is one of those names that are more popular than you think, in the Top 500 after ranking on the U.S. Top 1000 for nearly seventy years. It was first popularized via mid-century actor Dane Clark (born Bernard Zanville); actor and comedian Dane Cook gave it a more recent boost.

Dane is one of several rhyming cousins gaining in popularity — Zane, Thane, Cain/Kane — but not Wayne.

Dane also makes a great middle name, as evidenced by January Jones's use of it for son Xander Dane.

Daniel

Hebrew, "God is my judge"

Daniel is a perennial favorite. Though down from Number 10 to Number 11 this year, Daniel is one of only a handful of male names that sounds both classic and modern, strong yet approachable, and popular but not clichéd, with a solid Old Testament pedigree. The only real downside: there are more than 14,000 Daniels named each year, making it a less than distinctive choice.

Daniel was popular in the days of Daniel Webster and Daniel Boone, and its appeal is international, from Ireland to Israel. It was the name of one of the greatest biblical heroes, with the inspiring story of the prophet whose faith protected him when he was thrown into a den of lions, yet does not seem as solemn and weighty as others like Abraham and Ezekiel. And its nicknames — Danny and Dan — make it sound even friendlier; though, as with other classics, many modern parents are opting to use the name in full.

Daniel is currently the top name in Spain.

Darius

Roman from Persian, "protector"

Darius is a historic name via Emperor Darius the Great, a key figure in ancient Persian history, and several other Persian kings. His name today has an appealingly artistic image, which might well be found on a concert program or gallery announcement.

Among its cultural inspirations is composer Darius Milhaud. Journalist Christiane Amanpour, who was raised in Tehran, named her son Darius.

Darwin

English, "dear friend"

Darwin is a surprise millennial hero hit that has been on the popularity list since 2001. Enough parents have found naturalist Charles Darwin, the father of the theory of evolution, a worthy hero to keep it there — though some might just like its trendy two-syllable sound. It has a lovely meaning too — dear friend.

Dashiell

Anglicization of French surname de Chiel, meaning unknown

Dashiell, though missing from many other name sources, is among the hottest new names, chosen by such celebs as Cate Blanchett and author Helen (*Bridget Jones*) Fielding. With its great dash and panache, Dashiell is associated with detective writer Dashiell Hammett (born Samuel, as in Sam Spade, Dashiell being his mother's maiden name). Alice Cooper was ahead of the game: He named his son Dashiell in 1985.

And Dash is such a dashing nickname.

David

Hebrew, "beloved"

David is a classic with a lot going for it. Serious yet simpatico, it has deep biblical roots as the Hebrew name of the Old Testament second king of Israel who, as a boy, slew the giant Philistine Goliath with his slingshot, then grew up to become a wise and highly cultivated leader who enjoyed music and was a poet, later providing inspiration to such great sculptors as Michelangelo and Donatello.

David has a special resonance for Jews, the Star of David being the symbol of Judaism, while a sixth-century David became the patron saint of Wales, where it has always been a popular choice. David's a royal name well used in many cultures, and is a safe and timeless choice. The fact that it's still firmly in the Top 20 proves David's an enduring classic.

There have been countless Davids of note in history, entertainment, sport and fiction, including Copperfield, Crockett, Letterman and Beckham. Celebrities who have chosen it for their baby boys include Jennifer Hudson, Mo'Nique, and that incomparable name creator, J. K. Rowling. The increasingly popular Dawson means "son of David."

Davis

Surname derived from David, Hebrew, "beloved"

Davis is a fresh way to say David. Some sources define it as "son of David," but we see it as a surname spin on the original. While David is an everyman name, Davis has some creative edge — and still gets you to the classic guy nickname Dave.

Davis can be a good way to name a boy after grandpa David; Davies, Davison, or Davidson will also do the trick.

In the TV show *One Tree Hill*, the Sophie Bush character gives one of her twins her maiden name of Davis. Davis Guggenheim is an Oscar-winning director and documentarian, married to Elisabeth Shue.

Dawson

Welsh, "son of David"

Dawson was scarcely heard as a first name before the debut of *Dawson's Creek* in 1998, at which point it leaped up more than 550 places in one year. The character Dawson Leery, played by James Van Der Beek, was a teen favorite until the show's demise in 2003, but the name has retained its popularity, still at Number 315.

An offshoot of the David nickname Daw, Dawson could make a nice tribute to a namesake David. Also a common surname, there have been noted Dawsons from footballer Len to actress Rosario to the Leonardo DiCaprio character in *Titanic*, Jack Dawson.

In literature, Dawson Fairchild is a novelist character in William Faulkner's second novel, *Mosquitoes*.

Dax

French place-name

The appealingly energetic Dax, with its trendy "x" ending, has been on the popularity list for the past four years. Its somewhat sci-fi vibe emanates from his appearance as a fictional being in the Star Trek universe, seen on the TV show *Star Trek: Deep Space Nine*. The *Power Rangers* character Dax Lo was the Blue Ranger.

In real life, actor Dax Shepard plays the TV character of Crosby Braverman on *Parenthood*. His parents named him for the protagonist of the best-selling Harold Robbins novel, *The Adventurers* — Dax Xenos.

Dax is also a French community famous as a spa.

Declan

Irish, meaning unknown, possible "man of prayer"

Declan, the amiable and appealing name of an Irish saint (and the real first name of singer Elvis Costello), is very popular in the Emerald Isle and beginning its certain climb to popularity here, already at Number 143, after debuting on the American list in 1998 — it climbed 33 places in 2012. Like Aidan and Liam, Declan is shaping up to be an American hit.

St. Declan of Ardmore was a very early Irish missionary, preceding St. Patrick.

Cyndi Lauper spelled her son's name Declyn.

Denver

English or French place-name and surname, "green valley" or "from Anvers"

Before there was Aspen, Denver was the Colorado city name of choice, and we could see it resurfacing as a stylish two-syllable boys' name with the trendy "er" ending. Its decade of greatest use was the 1920s, when it reached as high as Number 422.

The one noted Denver was actor Denver Pyle, who played Uncle Jesse in *Dukes of Hazard*. The state capital was named for politician James W. Denver, and others who bore the surname were singer John (born John Deutschendorf), and Bob Denver, the face of *Gilligan Island*'s Gilligan.

Dermot

Anglicization of Diarmaid, Irish, "free man" or "free from envy"

Dermot is an appealing, relatively undiscovered Irish mythological hero's name long popular in the Old Country, and imported into the American consciousness by actor Dermot Mulroney. We see it in the next Celtic wave following Connor and Liam.

The name Dermot was borne by several early kings and a number of saints, as well as the legendary king of Tara. A further plus: The legendary Diarmaid (pronounced DEER-mit), a member of the band of Finn MacCool, had a mark on his face that caused women to fall instantly and madly in love with him.

Kermit the Frog owes his name to a regional variant of Dermot.

Desmond

Irish surname, "one from south Munster"

Desmond is a sophisticated and debonair name, with noble ties to 1984 Nobel Peace Prize-winning Bishop Desmond Tutu, and with some great nicknames — Des/Dez, Desi/Dezi. It is beginning to catch on in the US, now at Number 339.

Another notable Desmond is British zoologist and anthropologist Desmond Morris, author of *The Naked Ape* and other popular books.

The character Desmond David Hume on *Lost* was named in tribute to philosopher David Hume, and the name also appeared on *Oz;* Desmond Harrington plays Detective Joseph Quinn on *Dexter*.

And we can't forget all the references to Desmond in the Beatles song "Ob-La-Di, Ob-La-Da" — possibly used in tribute to reggae singer Desmond Dekker.

Devlin

Irish, "unlucky"

Devlin is an Irish name that's fresher and even more devilish than Devin.

The earliest written record of this surname occurs in the thirteenth century, when an O'Devlin was appointed Bishop of Kells in 1211.

In the contemporary world, Devlin Agamand is a character in the video game *War of Witchcraft* and there is a British rapper who goes by the single name Devlin. Bernadette Devlin was the youngest woman ever elected to the British Parliament.

Dex

Diminutive of Dexter, "dyer; right-handed"

Dex, the nickname for Dexter that is sometimes used on its own, has lots of energy and sex appeal. It was chosen by comedian Dana Carvey for his now-grown son. With the growing popularity of Dexter, we may be seeing more of Dex.

There are no less than three video game characters named Dex, and the leading male figure in the movie *One Day* is known by his nickname Dex. Way back in TV's *Dynasty* era, there was a character redundantly named Dex Dexter.

Dexter

Latin, "dyer, right-handed"

The jazzy, ultra-cool Dexter, like most names containing "x", has a lot of energy and sex appeal. Over the years, it's been attached to a number of diverse real and fictional personalities — C. K. Dexter Haven, the witty Cary Grant character in *The Philadelphia Story*, Dexter Green, the protagonist of the Scott Fitzgerald story *Winter Dreams*, great jazz tenor saxophonist Dexter Gordon and — oops — the current TV Dexter, who just happens to be a genial but sociopathic serial killer.

Dexter was chosen by hip musical couple Diana Krall and Elvis Costello for one of their twin boys, and by singer Charlotte Church.

Dexter has been climbing up the pop ladder, jumping 22 places in the past year, to reach Number 362. It is also in the Top 100 in the U.K.

Dex is an equally appealing nickname, now sometimes used on its own.

Dhani

Hindi, "rich"

Dhani is a haunting Indian name that's a million miles away from the similar sounding Danny. One notable namesake is musician Dhani Harrison, look-alike son of Beatle George. He is named after the sixth and seventh notes of the Indian music scale, "dha and "ni." "Dhani" is also a raga in north Indian classical music. Another noted bearer is longtime NFL linebacker Dhani Jones.

Dixon

Scottish, "son of Dick"

A relatively common surname, Dixon would be an inventive way to honor an ancestral Richard or Dick, the X form a lot livelier than the Dickson spelling, just as Dix is a more modern short form than Dick; it would be right at home alongside Dax and Jax.

And if Mason is among the hottest baby names — why not Dixon?

Django

Gypsy, "I awake"

Django — the *D* is silent as most everyone now knows — the nickname of the great Belgian-born jazz guitarist Django (originally Jean Baptiste) Reinhardt, makes a dynamic musical choice for any jazz aficionado. Reinhardt's nickname "Django" is Romani for "I awake." The name has become more familiar with the release of and acclaim for the Quentin Tarantino film *Django Unchained.*

Donovan

Irish, "dark"

One of the first of the appealing Irish surnames to take off in this country, Donovan has long outgrown its *Mellow Yellow* association, which came via the single from a 60s singer-songwriter named Donovan.

Donovan was Scottish-born Donovan Leitch, whose name was probably inspired by his father Donald's. He proved to be an adventurous, celestial namer himself — three of his children are Astrella Celeste, Oriole Nebula and Ione Skye.

Another potential namesake is Minnesota Vikings quarterback Donovan McNabb.

Donovan was in the Top 1000 as early as 1900, now ranking at Number 275.

Related options are surname Donegan and place name Donegal.

Dougal

Scottish, "dark stranger"

Heard in the Scottish highlands, and much more in tune with the present times than the dated Douglas — for which it could make a perfect tribute name — Dougal was the Scottish nickname for invading dark-haired Danish Vikings, just as Fingal was given to the blonder Norwegians.

Dougray, as in actor Dougray Scott, is a similarly appealing choice.

Drew

Diminutive of Andrew, "manly"

Drew, which projects a polished, somewhat intellectual impression, is rapidly becoming the Andrew nickname of choice, replacing the past favorite, Andy. It is fully capable of standing on its own, which it has for many decades, non-stop since 1942. It now ranks at Number 282.

There have been Drews in several iconic movies, such as *Deliverance* and *Steel Magnolias* and on TV in *Parenthood* and *Everybody Hates Chris*. High-profile Drews include Superbowl-winning Brees, comedian Carey and singer-songwriter Lachey. Drew Barrymore brought it over to the girls' side, but it has never ranked very high there.

Drummer

Occupational word name

Drummer entered the baby name lexicon thanks to blogger No Big Dill, when she chose it for her newborn son, who joins five older sisters. Drummer is right in step with other occupational names in vogue now, from Archer to Gardener. Let's just hope Drummer doesn't prefer to play the piano.

Dudley

English, "Dudda's meadow"

It's easy to love a name that rhymes with "cuddly" and is also attached to the surname Do-Right — once you ignore the "dud" connection.

Dudley has aristocratic roots — the name was originally famous via a sixteenth-century noble British family, one member of which, Robert Dudley, came close to marrying Queen Elizabeth I.

Dudley was the name of the angel played by Cary Grant in *The Bishop's Wife*, later remade with Denzel Washington in the role, while Dudley Dursley is a *Harry Potter* character. The name's most well-known bearer in modern times was comic actor Dudley Moore.

Duff

Irish, "swarthy"

This somewhat boisterous Celtic name would be at home in a noisy pub or out walking on the moors. In Scotland, it was originally a nickname for someone with dark hair or a swarthy complexion.

Duff (born Michael) McKagan gained fame as a member of Guns 'N' Roses. Popular actress Hilary Duff is giving the surname a lot of attention. Surname Duffy is another possibility.

Duncan

Scottish, "dark warrior"

Duncan is jaunty, confident, and open, a Scottish royal name that's brimming with friendly charm and makes it into our golden circle of names that are neither too popular nor too strange. Duncan has been a stalwart mid-list name, now at Number 799.

From a surname based on a clan name, Duncan was the name of a Scottish saint and two early Kings of the Scots. The beneficent Duncan I, who lived in the eleventh century, was immortalized in Shakespeare's *Macbeth*.

The brave and handsome Major Duncan Heyward is one of the main characters in James Fenimore Cooper's *The Last of the Mohicans*. Other cultural references include Duncan Idaho, the only character to appear in all of Frank Herbert's *Dune* novels, Duncan MacLeod, the immortal protagonist of *Highlander*, one of Garp's sons in *The World According to Garp*, and singer-songwriter Duncan Sheik.

David Bowie's son Zowie changed his name first to Joey and then finally to Duncan.

E

Eamon

Irish variation of Edmund, "wealthy protector"

This Irish name pronounced ay-mon was popularized in the US by early president of the independent republic Eamon de Valera (birth name George), who was born in the United States to an Irish mother and a Cuban father. Eamon definitely has possibilities as a successor to the epidemically popular Aidan/Aiden.

Though it may be an older generation name in Ireland, it would sound fresh elsewhere.

The original spelling of the name is Eamonn.

Easton

English, "east-facing place"

Easton is a stylish Ivy League-ish place and surname name, more modern than Weston, on its way up for both sexes as part of the new direction baby names are taking, as in North and West. Easton was used for her son by Jenna Elfman — and by Elizabeth Rohm for her daughter.

After entering the Top 1000 less than 20 years ago, Easton now stands in the Top 100.

Eben

Hebrew, diminutive of Ebenezer, "stone of help"

Though most parents would shy away from Ebenezer, short form Eben is affable and creative and perfectly able to stand alone; nothing Scroogish about it. This also makes a fresh new spin on the very popular Ethan or Evan.

Eben Oleson is the name of the character played by Josh Hartnett in the movie *30 Days of Night*.

Edison

English, "son of Edward"

This rhythmic last-name-first-name projects the creativity and inventiveness of Thomas A. Why is it suddenly being considered by new parents? A) They may possibly be inspired by the mega-trendy Addison, or B) influenced by the renewed interest in *Twilight* hero Edward and looking at other "Ed"-starting possibilities, or "C") attracted to the stylish "-son" ending, à la Jackson and Harrison.

Whatever the reason, Edison is rising through the ranks and strikes the perfect balance of familiar and distinctive.

Edmund

English, "wealthy protector"

The sophisticated Edmund and its nearly-identical French twin Edmond are coming out of mothballs now that Edward, inspired by *Twilight*, is once again a hot name.

Edmund has had an enviable history, as evidenced by these quotes: "There is nobleness in the name of Edmund," says a Jane Austen character, and the poet John Keats once bemoaned, "Had my name been Edmund, I would have been more fortunate."

Famous bearers include the English astronomer Edmond Halley, after whom the comet was named, poet Edmund Spenser, great Shakespearean actor Edmund Kean, and New Zealand mountaineer Sir Edmund Hillary. Literary Edmunds appear in *King Lear*, Jane Austen's *Mansfield Park*, and Dickens's *Little Dorrit*.

Edmund reached its highest point of popularity in the US in 1914, when it was Number 130; it hasn't appeared on the list since 1997 — making it even more attractive as an uncommon alternative to Edward.

Eamon is the cheery Irish version.

Edward

English, "wealthy guardian"

Unlike perennials William, John and James, Edward is a classic that moves in and out of fashion. This royal Anglo-Saxon standard is now benefiting from the popularity of the hot hero of the vampire sensation *Twilight*, Edward Cullen, who has given his name a new infusion of sex appeal.

Edward was the name of several Saxon and eight English kings, and is the name of the youngest son of the current queen. It was an early arrival in the New World — there were several Edwards in the Jamestown colony and six on the Mayflower.

Youngish actors Edwards Norton, Burns and Furlong help keep the name's image fresh. Parents today are more likely to prefer nicknames Ted or Ned to the traditional Ed or Eddie — or, just as likely, to use the name in full.

Egan

Irish, pet form of Aiden, "little fire"

Egan's likeness to the word eager gives this Irish surname a ready-to-please, effervescent energy, and it would make an appropriate substitute for the overused Aidan.

This popular Irish surname originated in County Tipperary.

Egan O'Rahilly (born Aogán Ó Rathaille) was the outstanding poet of his age, specializing in the vision poem, or aisling, in which he told of prophesies that Ireland would triumph over her enemies. In folklore, this Egan is depicted as a wise trickster.

Eleazar

Hebrew, "God is my helper"

Eleazar is a distinguished biblical name — in which it appears several times — ripe for the picking following the stardom of Eli, Elijah, and other similar names.

Eleazar is also a *Twilight* name, first appearing in the Stephanie Meyers book *Breaking Dawn*.

It's related most closely to Eliezer, which also appears in the Bible many times, as well as belonging to three great Talmudic scholars.

Eli

Hebrew, "ascended, uplifted, high"

Eli — a solid biblical name with lots of spirit and energy — is beginning to bound up the popularity charts, climbing 14 places in the last year to Number 44.

While Eli is a full name on its own, it can be a shortened form of Elijah, Eliezer, or even Elliot. CNN anchor Campbell Brown and SNL alum Rachel Dratch both chose Eli for their baby boys.

In the Old Testament, Eli was the high priest and last judge of Israel, who trained the prophet Samuel.

Elias

Greek, variation of Elijah, "Jehovah is God"

Elias, strong and charismatic, is following in the path of family members Elijah and Eli, and is also moving on up in popularity, nearing the Top 100.

Used by the English Puritans in the eighteenth century, Elias is the name of an oratorio about the prophet Elijah, composed by Felix Mendelssohn. There have been characters named Elias in novels by Sir Walter Scott, Anthony Trollope and Thomas Hardy. And in the inventors' Hall of Fame is Elias Howe, inventor of the sewing machine.

Elijah

Hebrew, "Jehovah is God"

Elijah — the name of the Old Testament prophet who went to heaven in a chariot of fire — has become a fashionable biblical choice. More than 13,000 parents chose Elijah last year, bringing it inside the Top 20 for the third year in a row — a possible challenge to Jacob for Number 1 in the future.

After long neglect, Elijah was suddenly rejuvenated when Cher and Greg Allman bestowed it on their son Elijah Blue in 1976, and got another shot of youth serum via young actor Elijah Wood.

Among other celebrities who have chosen Elijah for their boys are Donnie Wahlberg, James Spader, Tracy Nelson, Wynonna Judd and Bono (who followed it with middle names Bob Patricus Guggi G.).

Elijah figures in the Jewish, Christian and Muslim religions. There are numerous songs containing the name, and Elijah also figures in many books — including Charles Dickens's *Martin Chuzzlewit* — and in films.

Elio

Italian and Spanish from Greek sun god, Helios

Elio is a sunny and spirited Italian and Spanish name that makes a great crossover prospect, which could catch on as Enzo has. Elio is also currently popular in France, ranking in the Top 250.

Ellington

English place-name and surname, "Ellis's town"

Ellington is a swinging musical name, evoking the jazzy and elegant persona of the Duke (born Edward Kennedy Ellington). While that reference may seem to make Ellington a male name, it is also occasionally used for girls.

Ellington is the winning middle name of Cynthia Nixon's son Max.

Elliot

Anglicization of Elijah or Elias, "the Lord is my God"

Elliot (which boasts several spellings depending upon how many "l"s or "t"s you want to use) is a winner — it has the ideal quality of being neither too common nor weirdly unique. Elliot had a style boost back in the early 1980s via the young hero of the movie *E.T.*, who was named Elliot. Since then there have been Elliots on *Law & Order: SVU* and *Mad Men*.

Two of the name's spellings are running neck and neck: in 2012 Elliot was Number 242, Elliott 277. It is even more popular in England and Sweden.

Elliott namesakes include composer Carter, actor Gould, and photographer Elliott Erwitt.

Ellis

Welsh, "benevolent" or English surname derived from Elijah

Ellis is one of the less-used names in the currently popular "El" family. A popular Welsh name in its own right, sometimes spelled Elis, it may also be an English surname name derived from Elijah by way of Elias.

Ellis Bell was the male pseudonym of Emily Bronte when she wrote *Wuthering Heights*. Ellis Marsalis is the paterfamilias of the noted jazz family, father of Wynton, Bradford and others, and some might associate the name with Ellis Island, through which millions of immigrants entered the United States.

There have been a number of Ellises on the big and small screen — in *The Wire, Grey's Anatomy,* and *No Country for Old Men,* among others. As a surname it's associated with designer Perry, writer Bret Easton and psychologist Havelock.

There is currently a female character named Ellis on *Glee* — whether that will affect the perception of the name remains to be seen.

Elvis

Meaning unknown

When the King was alive, and for years afterwards, few people (except Declan MacManus who became Elvis Costello) dared use his singular name, but now it's very much up for grabs.

The name Elvis is connected to the Irish Ailbhe, and the Irish saint of that name is also known as Elvis of Munster.

Elvis was the middle name of the singer's dad, Vernon. Anthony Perkins, a big Elvis fan, gave the name to his now-grown son in 1976. Other aficionados, such as Cindy Crawford, have opted for the surname Presley.

Emilian

Romanian form of Emil, "rival"

With the new trend of boys' names rising on the heels of their popular sisters, the unusual-yet-familiar-feeling Emilian might become better known thanks to its relationship to Emily and Emilia/Amelia. Rather than being two branches of the same tree, Emilian and Emily are actually one tree while Emmett and Emma hang on a whole separate tree. But all have a lot of modern appeal, and Emilian may be a more attractive and intriguing male form than Emil. There was a St. Emilian.

Emmanuel

Hebrew, "God is with us"

Emmanuel — spelled with one or two "m"s — was popular with early Jewish immigrants, until overused nickname Manny caused it to fade. Now, this important biblical name is being revived in its full glory. In 2012, Emmanuel was Number 165, spelled Emanuel it was 306.

In the Bible, this is the name given to the promised Messiah, in the prophecy of Isaiah.

The name is popular in Spain as Manuel; the name of the German philosopher is spelled Immanuel Kant.

Emmett

Hebrew; English, "truth; universal"

Emmett, honest and sincere, laid-back and creative, is on the rise as a male cognate of the megapopular Emma and Emily, not to mention being a character in the popular *Twilight* series (Like Cullen, Emmett skyrocketed up more than 200 spots in 2009 and has since risen to Number 186). Emmett originated in England as a masculine diminutive of the German Emma and also means truth in Hebrew. Emmet is another, less popular spelling.

The death of young Emmett Till helped spark the civil rights movement.

Enzo

Italian, variation of Henry, also diminutive of Vincenzo and Lorenzo

Like Leonardo and Luca, Enzo, originally a short form of Vincenzo and Lorenzo, is one of the confident and captivating Italian names beginning to be used by parents of various ethnic backgrounds, including Patricia Arquette and Annabeth Gish.

In addition to its native country, Enzo is currently mega popular in France; and in the US it is now in the Top 500.

Sports car aficionados might associate the name with Enzo Ferrari, founder of the luxury brand.

Ephraim

Hebrew, "fruitful, fertile, productive"

Ephraim is an Old Testament name we would place high on the list of neglected biblical possibilities, solid but not solemn.

In Genesis, Ephraim is the second son of Joseph, and founder of one of the twelve tribes of Israel. The name also appears as characters in Oliver Goldsmith's *The Vicar of*

Wakefield and Dickens's novel *Little Dorrit* and in works by Sir Walter Scott and Robert Louis Stevenson. More recently, Ephraim Black was a character in the *Twilight* saga: a shape-shifter who was the great-grandfather of Jacob.

Father and son violinist and actor Efrem Zimbalist, Jr and Sr, simplified the spelling.

Erasmus

Greek, "beloved, desired"

Erasmus has long retained the image of the bearded and bespectacled Dutch philosopher, but could be one that the audacious baby namer just might dare to dust off.

The fourth-century Saint Erasmus was also known as Elmo, the patron saint of sailors. The name is closely associated with Renaissance humanist and theologian Desiderius Erasmus, who was born Geert Geerts.

Another less-known bearer was Charles Darwin's grandfather, the poet, naturalist and physician Erasmus Darwin. The fictional Erasmus Holyday is a learned teacher in Walter Scott's 1821 novel *Kenilworth*, published at a time when the name did have some popularity in England.

Ernest

English from German, "serious, resolute"

Ernest is one of those sober, so-far-out-they're-beginning-to-be-reconsidered Great Uncle names. It was a Top 40 name from 1880 to 1926, and has never been completely off the Social Security list.

Ernest is probably the only name a whole play was based on — Oscar Wilde's *The Importance of Being Earnest* — in which one character says "There is something in that name that seems to inspire absolute confidence. I pity any poor woman whose husband is not called Ernest." The most famous bearer of the name is Ernest Hemingway — unless you want to count Bert's friend Ernie.

Changing the spelling to Earnest makes it a male virtue name.

Esau

Hebrew, "hairy"

Esau is one of the neglected E-beginning boys' biblical choices — it's been off the popularity lists since 1902! The name of Jacob's twin brother, son of Isaac and Rebecca, Esau could make an ideal twin choice.

Kids might be familiar with the jingle "He saw Esau on the see-saw."

Evander

Latin form of Greek, "good man"

Evander is a name that could build on the popularity of shorter form Evan, and could work and play well with schoolmates like Zander and Xander.

Evander was prominent in Greek and Roman mythology: in classical lore Evander was a wise Arcadian hero who founded the city in Italy that preceded Rome, appearing in Virgil's *Aeneid*.

In modern times, the name has been associated with boxing champ Evander Holyfield.

Evander could make a more distinctive alternative to Alexander.

Everest

Place-name, world's tallest mountain

A twist on the standard Everett takes it to lofty heights. The snow-capped Everest would surely stand out in a classroom, yet has an acceptable name-like feel. George Lucas bestowed it on his daughter, but it still feels very male to us.

Everett

English variation of the German Eberhard, "brave as a wild boar"

Everett is a statesmanlike, wintry New England name chosen by over a thousand parents each year. In the past three years, Everett shot up 106 spots to Number 214, a fashion leap that can be credited to its similarity to trendy girls' names such as Eva and Ava. Its high point was about a century ago, when Everett was a Top 100 name — and it could get there again.

Everett Hills is a character in Eugene O'Neill's drama *Mourning Becomes Electra*. Author John Irving named his youngest son Everett.

Ewan

Scottish form of Gaelic Eoghan, "born of the yew tree"

This appealing name has a good chance of catching on due to the popularity of Ewan McGregor, and the trend towards Gaelic names in general. Pronunciation is YOO-un.

Ewan has a complex family tree, with connections to John, Owen, Hugh, Evan and Eugene. Other spellings are Ewen, Eoin and Euan.

In Willa Cather's novel *My Mortal Enemy*, there is a character called Ewan Gray.

Ezekiel

Hebrew, "God strengthens"

Ezekiel, a visionary Old Testament prophet name, used to be reduced to its nickname Zeke, but modern parents now embrace it in full for its power and dignity. Along with biblical brethren Asher and Ezra, Ezekiel is rising steadily up the popularity charts and is poised to take over for fading first wave Old Testament choices such as Zachary. Ezekiel now ranks in the Top 200, close to the highest it's ever been, representing nearly 2,000 boys.

Both Beau Bridges and Tisha Campbell Martin have sons named Ezekiel.

Ezra

Hebrew, "help"

Ezra has a lot going for it: the strength of its heroic biblical legacy, its quirky sound, and its fresh but familiar feel. Ezra is currently growing in popularity with parents seeking a less popular biblical name — it is now at Number 184 — its highest ever.

According to the Bible, Ezra led a group of fifteen hundred Israelites out of slavery in Babylon and back to Jerusalem. There is also the poetry connection to Ezra Pound — in addition to young Washington Post blogger Ezra Klein. Ezra Cornell was a founder of Western Union and co-founder of the university that bears his name and Ezra Jack Keats is a popular children's book author-illustrator.

Both Paul Reiser and Taylor Hanson are dads to boys named Ezra, and there are Ezras to be found in Wilkie Collins's *The Moonstone* and *Daniel Deronda* by George Eliot.

And let's not forget the band — Better Than Ezra — or rising actor Ezra Miller.

F

Farrell

Irish, "courageous"

If you're looking for a pleasing namesake that's more modern than Darrell/Darryl, this would make an excellent choice. Farrell is an Anglicized form of the Irish Fergal, and was well used as a first name into the nineteenth century, before it faded to mostly surname use.

Irish actor Colin Farrell gives the name a big, bold shot of bravura; other notable last-named Farrells include operatic soprano Eileen, *Studs Lonigan*-author James T., ballerina Suzanne, and rocker Perry of Jane's Addiction.

Felix

Latin, "happy"

Felix, energetic and upbeat with a felicitous meaning, has finally transcended its negative associations to Felix the Cat and the persnickety Felix Unger.

The name of four popes and sixty-seven saints, Felix has long been fashionable in upscale London and is rapidly becoming a Nameberry fave. The name was first adopted by the ancient Roman Sulla, who believed that he was especially blessed with luck by the gods. In the Bible, Felix is a Roman procurator of Judea.

The name appears in literature as the central character in George Eliot's novel *Felix Holt*, the protagonist of Thomas Mann's *Confessions of Felix Krull*, in Thomas Hardy's *Tess of the D'Urbervilles*, Henry James's *The Europeans*, Kurt Vonnegut's *Cat's Cradle*, and as a member of the Volturi Guard in the *Twilight* series. In movies Felix has popped up in everything from several James Bond films to *Spy Kids* and *The Hangover*.

Gillian Anderson and Elizabeth Banks are two modern celebrities who chose Felix for their baby boys. A notable namesake is Felix Frankfurter, a long-term Supreme Court Justice.

Popular in the Hispanic community, Felix is also celebrating a surge in Germany and Austria, where it is in the Top 15. Felix has been on the US popularity list for as long as records have been kept, now at Number 316.

Fergus

Scottish and Irish, "man of force"

In Celtic lore, Fergus was the ideal of manly courage; Fergus is a charming, slightly quirky Scottish and Irish favorite.

As a name, Fergus forms a link between Ireland and Scotland, as Gaelic tradition has it that Irish Prince Fergus Mac Eirc and his two brothers crossed the sea and founded the kingdom of Argyll in Scotland, thereby making this an excellent choice for parents of either or a combined heritage.

Fergus has often popped up in children's literature, such as in *Thomas the Tank Engine and Friends*, and is the name of one of Shrek and Fiona's triplets. On a loftier level, there is the Yeats poem, "*Who Goes With Fergus?*".

With the nickname Fergie having been appropriated by two high-profile females, we'd opt for using Gus instead.

Field

Nature name

More unusual than Forest or Forrest, Field is a nature name that is simple, evocative, and fresh — sort of the male equivalent of Meadow.

Field and Fields are both relatively common surnames, noted bearers including department store owner Marshall Field, poet Eugene Field ("Wynken, Blynken, and Nod") and actress Sally. Those with the plural include W.C. Fields, cookie company founder Debbi, and entertainers Gracie and Kim Fields.

Fielding is a very usable extension.

Finian

Irish, "fair"

This lilting Irish saint's name shone in neon lights on Broadway for the classical 1947 musical *Finian's Rainbow*, later made into a film starring Fred Astaire as Finian McLonergan, and there was also a character on *General Hospital* named Finian O'Toole. With the growing popularity of Finn and Finlay/Finley — and boys' names ending in "an" — Finian, which can also be spelled Finnian, seems like a sure-fire winner.

One of several early St. Finnians was a noted teacher and scholar.

Finlay

Irish and Scottish, "fair-haired hero"

Finlay is a formerly fusty Scottish royal name — it belonged to Macbeth's father, Finlay

MacRory — or Findlaech mac Ruaidri — that has a bit of a split personality. It has two acceptable spellings — Finlay and Finley, the first more popular in its native Scotland, where it ranks in the Top 20, with Finley vastly more popular in the US. While the Finlay spelling is given to twice as many boys as girls in the U.S., the balance is shifting girlward, taking both spellings into account.

Increasingly popular on the celebrity circuit, the splits are evident here too. Amanda Pays and Corbin Bernsen, and Sadie Frost have boys named Finlay, Chris O'Donnell and Holly Marie Combs have sons called Finley, and Lisa Marie Presley, Daniel Baldwin, and Angie Harmon and Jason Sehorn have daughters named Finley; the latter couple was instrumental in making the gender switch in 2003.

Finn

Irish, "white, fair"
Finn is a name with enormous energy and charm, that of the greatest hero of Irish mythology, Finn MacCool (aka Fionn mac Cuumhaill), an intrepid warrior with mystical supernatural powers, noted as well for his wisdom and generosity.

Finn is rising fast through the charts and is a Nameberry favorite — and is also (go figure) the fourth most popular name in Germany. After entering the U.S. pop list in 2000, Finn has moved up every year since, now at Number 291.

Finn was chosen by cool couple Christy Turlington and Ed Burns for their son, and also by Jane Leeves and Autumn Reeser. Finn Hudson was a prominent character on *Glee*.

Other up-and-comers in the same family: Finlayand Finley, Finian and Finnian, Finnegan and Finnigan, and, from Germany, Fynn.

Finnegan

Irish, "fair"
If you like the Finn names and love James Joyce, Finnegan is extremely winning. *Will & Grace's* Eric McCormack chose the Finnigan spelling for his son. And of course Finnegan gains you access to the great short form Finn.

James Joyce took the title of *Finnegan's Wake* from an old Dublin ballad.

Finnegan represents a whole genre of Irish family names you might consider, such as Harrigan, Brannigan, Corrigan, Donegan, Mulligan, Flanagan, Lanigan, and more.

Fiorello

Italian, "little flower"
Fiorello is one of the few floral names that work well for a boy. The colorful three-term

World War II New York Mayor La Guardia made this one famous — in fact he was nicknamed "the Little Flower." His life was the basis for the 1959 musical called, appropriately, *Fiorello!*

The Spanish version is Florencio.

Fisher

Occupational name, "fisherman"
As a member of two trendy name categories, animal and occupational, this name broke into the Top 1000 in 2004, and would make a nice tribute to an angler Grandpa.

The best known bearer, Fisher Stevens, pulled a switcheroo on his birth name Steven Fisher. Fischer (another possible spelling) Black was a distinguished economist.

Fisher is a fairly common surname, whose bearers include the family of Eddie, Carrie and Joely, actress Isla, food writer M.F.K. Fisher, and two legendary cartoonists: Bud Fisher, creator of "Mutt 'n' Jeff," and Ham Fisher, who invented Joe Palooka.

Fletcher

English, "arrow-maker"
Fletcher is a common surname with a touch of quirkiness; it definitely fits into the so-far-out-it's-in category — and moving further in all the time along with other occupational names from Parker to Forester.

One notable historical Fletcher is Fletcher Christian, the British seaman and mutineer portrayed on the screen at various times by Errol Flynn, Clark Gable, Marlon Brando and Mel Gibson. A musical namesake is Fletcher Henderson, who was important in the development of big band jazz and swing music.

Flint

English, "born near outcrop of flint"
Flint is one of the new macho names on the rise today, part old-school tough guy, part rebel. You won't find a tougher, steelier-sounding name; it's part of a genre on the rise along with cousins Slate, Stone and Steel.

Flint found itself on the popularity list for a few years in 1959-60, but would prove a distinctive choice today.

Flint has superhero overtones — there's one in *Spiderman* — aka Sandman — and Captain Flint was a Marvel comic, as well as a Robert Louis Stevenson character. But on the softer side, there's also inventor Flint Lockwood in *Cloudy With a Chance of Meatballs.*

Florian

Latin, "flowering"

If Flora and Florence have returned full force, Florian, with its trendy Latinate ending, could also have a chance. Popular in Germany, Austria and Switzerland — he was the venerated patron saint of those in danger from water and of firefighters — might sound a tad feminine and floral to English speakers. But as a middle name, Florian could be a great way to honor grandma Florence (or any other flower name).

The second-century Roman martyr St. Florian appears in Tennyson's poem *The Princess*, and also in Gilbert & Sullivan's comic opera *Princess Ida*. Sir Florian Eustace is an off-stage character in Trollope's novel *The Eustace Diamonds*, Florian Fortescue runs an ice cream shop in *Harry Potter*, and Florian is the real first name of singer Dido.

Floyd

Welsh, "gray-haired"

Floyd was a Top 100 name from the 1880s to the 1940s that somehow developed an almost comical hayseed persona along with a touch of retro jazz cool; it just might appeal to parents with a strong taste for the quirky.

In terms of namesakes and references, there is two-time heavyweight champ Floyd Patterson, well-known attorney Floyd Abrams, Mayberry barber Floyd Lawson, Muppet Floyd Pepper, and the iconic British rock band, Pink Floyd.

Flynn

Irish, "son of the red-haired one"

Flynn, a charming Irish surname, is still used only quietly, despite its easygoing, casual cowboy charm, unlike Finn which is a star of this genre. Flynn was the choice of Orlando Bloom and Miranda Kerr for their baby boy, and is also the middle name — used as his first — of a son of Miranda's fellow supermodel Elle Macpherson, of Gary Oldman's son Gulliver, and Marley Shelton's daughter West.

Flynn Rider (born Eugene Fitzherbert) is the dashing animated hero of the Disney film *Tangled*. The name was long associated with the swashbuckling Errol Flynn, inspiration of the phrase "in like Flynn."

Flynn entered the US Top 1000 in 2011, and is a Top 100 choice in Australia and New Zealand.

Ford

English, "dweller at the ford"

The long association to the Ford Motor Company doesn't stand in the way of this being a strong, independent, single-syllable name.

Owen Wilson named his son Robert Ford — although the baby's name was first released as Ford Linton.

Among notable namesakes are writer Ford Madox Ford, author of *The Good Soldier*, who was born Ford Hermann Hueffer but changed his Germanic name to honor his grandfather, the pre-Raphaelite painter Ford Madox Brown; and sportswriter Ford Frick, who was elected to the Baseball Hall of Fame.

There are many more outstanding surnamed-Fords, including the presidential Gerald (born Leslie Lynch King, Jr) and his wife Betty, industrialist Henry and actor Harrison, to name a few.

Ford can work on its own or be a short form of a name such as Clifford.

Forrest

English, "dweller near the woods"
Forrest is one of the earliest appealingly sylvan, outdoorsy choices, borne by newsman Sawyer, actor Forest Whitaker, and football Hall of Famer Gregg. Forrest Gates was a character on *Buffy the Vampire Slayer*.

Forrest was steadily on the US popularity list until 2003, reaching a high of Number 175 in 1913, and then receiving a somewhat surprising blip after the release of *Forrest Gump*.

Early Forrests were named in honor of Confederate General Nathan Bedford Forrest, head of a famous cavalry force, who advised "Git there fuster with the mostest men."

Foster

Occupational name, "forester"
Foster is one commonly heard last name that makes a fine first. More unusual than Forrester or Gardener yet eminently first-name-ready, the only problem with Foster might be its association with "foster child."

There are numerous notable last-named Fosters, including composer Stephen, actresses Jodie and Sutton, architect Norman, and comic strip artist Hal, creator of *Prince Valiant*.

Fox

Animal name
Fox is one animal name backed by a longish tradition, and then popularized via the lead character Fox Mulder on *The X-Files*. Fox is simple, sleek, and a little bit wild, and could make an interesting middle name.

It was reported that the TV character's first name was not a tribute to the Fox network which aired *The X-Files*, as often assumed; show creator Chris Carter said he had a childhood friend named Fox.

Francis

Latin, "Frenchman" or "free man"
Now that this is the name that was chosen by the current Roman Catholic pope, Francis has come into the spotlight.

In fact, this name, which was in the Top 10 at the turn of the last century, has been pretty much confined to Irish and Italian Catholics (think F. [Francis] Scott Fitzgerald, Francis Albert Sinatra, Francis Ford Coppola) for decades, and still has a somewhat starchy feel. But with its similarity to the increasingly popular female Frances, and its recent newsworthiness, we can see it making a possible comeback beyond those worlds.

Animal-loving parents might be inspired by the connection to Saint Francis of Assisi (born Giovanni), who was said to be able to communicate with animals and was made the patron saint of ecology. Another Francis, Saint Francis de Sales, is the patron saint of writers and editors.

Frank

Diminutive of Francis or Franklin, "Frenchman" or "free man"
A Top 10 name from the 1880s until the 1920s, Frank has fallen from favor but still has a certain warm, friendly real-guy grandpa flavor that could come back into style, like other such choices as Jake and Jack. Maybe thanks to Sinatra, it's become a new hipster favorite with such couples as Diana Krall and Elvis Costello.

Frank has a wide variety of interesting namesakes, including architects Frank Lloyd Wright and Frank Gehry, artist Frank Stella, director Frank Capra, musician Frank Zappa, and Muppeteer director Frank Oz, to name a few.

Fred

German, diminutive of Frederick and Alfred
Where have all the Freds gone? We haven't seen many since the days of Flintstone and Munster. But it could be time for a comeback — if you think more of the sophistication of Fred Astaire, and of other nice guy names like Jack and Charlie and Sam.

Fred dropped off the popularity list in 2002, after being a double-digit favorite until 1955. Fred Weasley is a *Harry Potter* character, and on current TV, there are Freds on *Mad Men* and *Hot in Cleveland*.

Frederick

German, "peaceful ruler"

Frederick, and friendlier nickname Fred, seemed almost to have disappeared, leaving just the memory of Freds past such as Astaire, Mr. Rogers and Flintsone, but today's parents are beginning to recognize it as a strong classic to reconsider.

Previously, Frederick had taken on a rather forbidding, foreign, military air, reminiscent of Frederick the Great, the enlightened King of Prussia who laid the foundations of the powerful Prussian empire.

For African-Americans, Frederick can be seen as a hero name, honoring Frederick Douglass, who rose from slavery to power as a political activist.

Frederick appears as a character in Shakespeare's *As You Like It*, and the novels of, among others, Jane Austen and Henry James. The name is often streamlined to Frederic and even Fredric, and if you don't like Fred or Freddie (though we do), another nickname is Fritz.

Federico is the appealing Italian and Spanish form, as in renowned poet Federico Garcia Lorca.

Fritz

German, diminutive of Friedrich or Frederick, "peaceful ruler"

Since female cousins Mitzi and Fritzi have entered the realm of possibility, there's a chance that Cousin Fritz could as well. Fritz is the name of several notables, from early German-born film director Lang to early footballer Fritz (born Frederick) Pollard, the first African-American to play in the Rose Bowl in 1916.

Fritz has several other pop culture references, including the R. Crumb comic strip *Fritz the Cat*, begun in 1965 and which became a popular animated feature seven years later, and as one of the children in both *The Nutcracker* and *Swiss Family Robinson*. Fritz is also the nickname of former vice president Walter Frederick Mondale.

Frost

English surname, "white-haired, born in a cold spell"

Long heard as a last name, as in venerable poet Robert, U.K. talk show host David, British actress Sadie and old Jack Frost, the personification of cold winter weather, Frost has suddenly entered the scene as a possible first, along with other seasonal weather names like Winter and Snow.

Some forward-thinking parents are beginning to warm to the icy simplicity of Frost.

G

Gable

French, "triangular feature in architecture"
The iconic *Gone With the Wind* star Clark's surname was brought into the first-name mix when *Weeds'* Kevin Nealon picked it for his son. Gable makes a strong and unusual possibility, a rhyming cousin to Abel and Mable.

The cast of Golden Age and later Hollywood characters is ever increasing, now including Harlow, Chaplin, Flynn and Monroe.

Gage

French, "oath, pledge"
Gage, part of the current craze for one-syllable surnames, is hovering around the Top 150, with associations to tasty green gage plums and the mathematical gauge.

Gage was first noticed as a character in Stephen King's *Pet Sematary* — though Gage Creed was far from an admirable role model. That book was published in 1983, and the movie came out in 1989, the very year that Gage hit the Top 1000. It is now at Number 172, and there were more than 2,000 little Gages born in 2012.

Gage has spawned a couple of successful spelling variations, so don't be surprised to run into a Gaige or a Gauge.

Galway

Place-name
Associated with the poet and novelist Galway Kinnell, this name of an Irish town, county, and bay would make an evocative choice. For further literary cred, writers Liam O'Flaherty and Frank Harris both hail from Galway.

Galway has several sister cities in the U.S., including Chicago, Seattle, Milwaukee and St. Louis. A few other Irish place name possibilities: Dublin, Ennis, Donegal, Carlow, Tralee and Derry.

Gardener

English, "keeper of the garden"

Gardener is surely one of the most pleasant and evocative of the occupational options, calling up images of green grass and budding blooms. The name can also be spelled without the first "e," as in Gardner (born George Cadogan Gardner) McCay, a hunky TV heartthrob of the 1950s and 60s. Gardner is a much more common surname spelling, associated with screen legend Ava, mystery writer Erle Stanley and art collector and patron Isabella Stewart, founder of Boston's Gardner Museum.

Gareth

Welsh, "gentle"

Gareth, the name of a modest and brave knight in King Arthur's court, makes a sensitive, gently appealing choice, used more in its native Wales than anywhere else.

The name Gareth first appeared in Malory's *Morte d'Arthur*, as the lover of Eluned, the brother of Gawain and nephew of King Arthur. He also appears in the Gareth and Lynette segment of Tennyson's *Idylls of the King*. In the British version of *The Office*, Gareth is the name of the equivalent character of Dwight Schrute, and it also appeared in *Four Weddings and a Funeral*. Recommended nickname: Gaz. Not recommended nickname: Gary.

Gatsby

German surname and literary name

Suddenly, we're hearing the name Gatsby, as in *The Great* character by F. Scott Fitzgerald, used as a first name for girls as well as boys. The book's Jay Gatsby gussied up his name from Gatz, whose meaning is given variously as left-handed, cat, God, and person from Gat. As a first name, it's got a lot of energy and that great pedigree.

Gavin

Celtic, "white hawk"

Gavin, a name with Scottish roots, has stepped into the spotlight, replacing the dated Kevin, thanks in part to pop-rock sensation Gavin DeGraw and Bush lead singer Gavin Rossdale.

Gavin also has made literary appearances in J.M. Barrie's *The Little Minister* and in William Faulkner's Snopes family trilogy. In the form Gawain, he was one of the Knights of King Arthur's Round Table.

Gavin entered the ranks in the 1950s and has had a spectacular recent rise, in the Top 40 since 2006.

George

Greek, "farmer"

With the announcement of the new little British prince's name choice, the spotlight has focused on this vintage classic — but we've always been fans.

Yes, iconoclasts though we may be, we like Fred, we like Frank, and we like George, which was among the Top 10 from 1830 to 1950, when the number of little Georges started to decline. Solid, strong, royal and saintly, yet friendly and unpretentious, we think that George is in prime position for a comeback, especially with the recent attention it's received — like its sister Georgia.

George was the name of the king of Britain for 116 straight years, as well as the patron saint of England, Saint George, who, by slaying the dragon, became the symbol of good conquering evil. America's most famous George is, of course, Washington, the Father of Our Country.

Just a few of the many, many possible namesakes are George Handel, Shaw, Bush, Gershwin, Burns, Clooney, Shearing, Steinbrenner, Stephanopoulos, Harrison, Orwell, McGovern, Lucas and Clooney.

Celebrities who have chosen George for their sons include Kristin Scott Thomas, Jane Kaczmarek and Eva Herzigova. George Forman named all five of his sons George.

Not surprisingly, there are Georges scattered through English and American literature, including in two Jane Austen novels, and in *Vanity Fair, Uncle Tom's Cabin* and *An American Tragedy*, not to mention *Curious George, George of the Jungle*, George Jetson, George Jefferson, George Bailey and George Costanza.

Giacomo

Italian variation of James, "supplanter"

Giacomo is a primo member of the Giovanni-Gino-Giancarlo-Giacomo gruppo of Italian names that are beginning to be adopted by American parents. Singer/creative baby namer Sting chose it for his son.

Giacomo has many notable native namesakes, including composer Puccini, lothario Casanova, and poet Leopardi.

Gideon

Hebrew, "hewer; or, having a stump for a hand"

Gideon is an unjustly neglected Old Testament name — which has just recently started to climb — is an excellent choice for parents looking to move beyond such overused biblicals as Benjamin and Jacob. In the Old Testament, Gideon was a judge called on by

God to rescue the Jews from the Midianites, and the name was popular among the Puritans.

Gideon, now finally in the Top 500, was given a spike by the short-lived TV series *Gideon's Crossing*, and has been heard more recently as a main character in *Criminal Minds*, as Molly Weasley's brother Gideon Prewett in the *Harry Potter* series, and as an anti-hero, Gideon Gordon Graves, in the *Scott Pilgrim* series.

Among the celebs who have chosen Gideon for their sons are Neil Patrick Harris and Ziggy Marley.

Gilbert

German, "shining pledge"
Considered ultradebonair in the silent-movie era, Gilbert then went through a nerdy phase, a la Gilbert Gottfried. Now though, like Albert and Alfred and Walter and Frank, it could be in for a style revival.

Gilbert has been on the U.S. popularity list for centuries, reaching as high as Number 121 in the 1900s. The Normans introduced Gilbert to England, where it was common during the Middle Ages; it was the name of a twelfth-century English saint.

Gilberts have appeared in such books as Henry James's *Portrait of a Lady*, *Anne of Green Gables* and Ayn Rand's *Atlas Shrugged*, and on screen in *The Incredibles*, and as embodied by the young Johnny Depp in *What's Eating Gilbert Grape?* The most famous portrait painter of George Washington was Gilbert Stuart.

Nickname Gil could come back along with Hal, but even more appealing is Gib or Gibby.

Giulio

Italian variation of Julius, "youthful, downy-bearded"
Since the female Giulia and Giada have crossed the Atlantic, we think brother Giulio is a good candidate to follow, being more manageable than the longer (but equally attractive) Giuliano, Giovanni and Giacomo.

Gordon

Scottish, "great hill"
As this long-term Age of Jordans, both male and female, begins to wind down, the neglected Scottish favorite Gordon, with its more distinguished history, could come back as a distinctive alternative. Originally a surname, it was used in honor of nineteenth-century general Charles George Gordon, killed defending the city of Khartoum. Conservative but not stodgy, Gordon was a Top 100 name from 1911 to 1943, but has been completely out of the Top 1000 since 2008.

A contemporary political headliner is former Prime Minister Gordon Brown (born James Gordon), and other distinguished bearers of the name have been photographer and film director Parks, Scottish celebrity chef Ramsay, and the beloved *Sesame Street* character Gordon Robinson. We won't even mention that symbol of corporate greed — Gordon Gekko.

Gower

Welsh, "pure"

This Old Welsh name associated with blacksmiths has never caught on, but it has the right two-syllable occupational feel to qualify for revival. Gower Champion was a successful mid-century dancer, choreographer, and director on the Broadway stage, in films and on TV.

Grady

Irish, "noble, illustrious"

Following in the footsteps of popular brother Brady, Grady is another lively, ebullient Irish surname name. The O'Gradys (originally O Gradaugh) were an ancient clan which produced an impressive number of bishops.

Cleveland Indian outfielder Grady Sizemore was born Gradius.

Graham

Scottish, "gravelly homestead"

Well used in England and Scotland since the 50s, the smooth and sophisticated Graham is just beginning to catch on here; Graham has climbed almost 200 places in a decade.

Among the best known bearers are novelist Graham Greene, racing driver Graham Hill and painter Graham Sutherland, as well as musicians Graham Nash and Parker — and Gram Parsons.

The Scots sometimes spell it Graeme, and the Brits use Gram as its nickname.

Granger

English occupational name, "worker of the granary"

If you're seeking a solid last-name-first occupational name with a warm, friendly sound, one that's not overused, this could be it.

Granger is much better known as a surname — think handsome mid-century actors Stewart and Farley, and, more recently and majorly, Hermione Jean Granger, one of the three main protagonists of the *Harry Potter* series — but would make an unusual but accessible first.

Gray

Color name, also diminutive of Grayson

The girls have Violet and Scarlet and Ruby and Rose, but for the boys there's a much more limited palette of color names. Gray (or Grey), is one exception, which could make for a soft and evocative — if slightly somber — choice, especially in the middle. Kaitlin Olson and Rob McElhenney recently named their son Leo Grey.

A common surname, Gray/Grey is still an unusual first name choice — it hasn't made it into the Top 1000 in this century — while longer forms Grayson and Greyson are climbing rapidly, with Grayson in the Top 100 and his twin in the Top 200.

The best known bearer of the name, former Governor Gray Davis of California, was born Joseph Graham Davis, Jr, and others with Gray names include Graydon Carter (born Edward Graydon), editor of *Vanity Fair*, and Grayer, the child in *The Nanny Diaries*.

And we can't not mention the protagonist of the sensational bestselling erotic romance *50 Shades of Grey* — Christian Grey.

Grayson

English, "the son of the bailiff"

Grayson, which you might think of as a Jason-Mason substitute, is on the fast track. Though — you may be surprised to know — Grayson has been in the Top 1000 since 1984, it is now at its highest point ever, at Number 85 and climbing.

Some parents are even adopting Grayson — or Gracen or Gracyn — for girls as an androgynous spin on Grace. Greyson is an alternate spelling which, at Number 174, isn't lagging far behind Grayson. The name of the child in *The Nanny Diaries* is Grayer, and actor Tyler Christopher opted for the unusual spelling of Greysun for his son.

Griffin

Welsh, variation of Griffith, "strong lord"

Griffin is one of the newer and most appealing of the two-syllable Celtic surnames (also the name of a mythological creature, half-eagle, half-lion). It entered the list in 1983 after an absence of 75+ years, and has been climbing ever since, now at Number 220.

Brendan Fraser, Teri Polo and Joey McIntyre all chose Griffin for their sons. Actor Griffin Dunne's mother's maiden name was Griffin. Another well-known bearer was Griffin Bell, Jimmy Carter's Attorney General.

Also worth considering: the original classic Welsh Griffith.

Grover

English, "lives near a grove of trees"

Forget the furry blue Muppet, forget corpulent President Cleveland (not too difficult), and consider this name anew. We think it's spunky, a little funky, and well worth a second look.

President (Stephen) Grover Cleveland is actually a more than respectable namesake. The only president to serve two non-consecutive terms, he was well liked and respected. Many children were named in his honor, including the major league Hall of Fame pitcher Grover Cleveland Alexander. Another well-known Grover is jazz saxophonist Grover Washington Jr.

Not surprisingly, Grover was at its most popular as a baby name around the time of Cleveland's presidency; it was Number 20 in 1884 and 1885.

Gulliver

Irish, "glutton"

Gulliver is an obscure Gaelic surname known almost solely through its literary *Travels* until actor Gary Oldman used it for his son, instantly transforming it into a lively option. British actors Damian Lewis, of *Homeland*, and Helen McCrory also have a son named Gulliver.

Gunther

German, "bold warrior"

When it's spelled with two dots over the "u" in German, Gunther is pronounced GUWN-ter, but it has a much softer sound when the "h" is voiced by English-speakers, as it was, for example, for the name of a character in *Friends*.

Gunther has never been as well used in this country as the Scandinavian version, Gunnar, which now ranks at Number 502, making Gunther all the more distinctive.

Well-known Gunthers include German novelist Gunt(h)er Grass and the character in the German epic poem *Die Nibelungenlied*, which formed the basis for Richard Wagner's Ring cycle of operas.

Gus

Diminutive of Augustus, Angus, Gustave, Augustin, Augusten, Augustine, August

Gus is a homey grandpa nickname name that can work as a short form for any of the above or stand on its own as a cutting-edge replacement for Max and Jake — though it dropped off the Top 1000 in 1978.

Gus was chosen for their sons by Dixie Chick Emily Robison and actress Julie Bowen. In T.S. Eliot's *Old Possum's Book of Practical Cats* (and in the stage musical), the full name of Gus the Theatre Cat is Asparagus.

Guthrie

Scottish, "windy spot"

Guthrie, an attractive Irish surname-name, has a particularly romantic, windswept aura, with a touch of the buckaroo thrown in.

Guthrie's folkie quality is tied to the father and son pair of singers Woody (born Woodrow Wilson) and Arlo. Other Guthries: Guthrie McClintic, a major figure in the Broadway theatre world of the early twentieth century, and Guthrie Govan, a guitarist with Asia and other bands.

H

Hal

Diminutive of Harold and Henry

Could Hal be the Jack, Max, or Gus of the future? It just might happen in the new nickname environment. Hank Azaria put it on his son's birth certificate.

Hal is a venerable nickname for Henry, Harry and Harold, famously used by Shakespeare in *King Henry IV* as the name of the king's son, the future Henry V.

A number of show biz figures of a certain era have gone by the name, including Hals Roach, Wallis, Ashby, Holbrook, David and Linden. In the eponymous film, Jack Black played *Shallow Hal*.

As for the bad-guy machine in *2001: A Space Odyssey*, that HAL stood for Heuristically programmed ALgorithmic computer.

Hamish

Scottish variation of James, "supplanter"

Just as Seamus/Seumus is Irish for James, Hamish is the Scottish form — one that's not often used here, but still redolent of Olde Scotland. If you're ready to go further than Duncan and Malcolm, out to Laird and Ewan territory, this may be worth consideration. It also sounds just like the Yiddish word for homey.

In Scotland, where it became popular in the second half of the nineteenth century, Hamish is a nickname for a Highlander, and it's a high-ranking name in South Australia, where it's currently in the Top 50.

Some people may have become familiar with Hamish via one of the grooms in *Four Weddings and a Funeral*.

Hank

Diminutive of Henry, German, "estate ruler"

Hank is a mid-century guy nickname (which actually dates back to the seventeenth century) of the Al/Hal/Dick school, which has been on recess from the playground for decades. Now it's just beginning to be given on its own again, appreciated for its earthy, sportsguy cool. Hanks Aaron and Greenberg (born Henry) and Hank Williams (born Hiram) Sr and Jr are worthy namesakes.

Kendra Wilkinson named her little boy Hank IV.

Hardy

German, "bold, brave"
Hardy is a spirited and durable un-Germanic German surname name that is starting to be used in this country.

British fashion designer Hardy Amies (born Edwin) is its best known bearer, and Thomas Hardy could make a literary namesake — as might the old *Hardy Boys* series of adventure books for young boys.

Harrison

English, "son of Harry"
Harrison, a name made viable by Harrison Ford, is increasingly popular with parents who want an H name that's more formal than Harry or Hank but doesn't veer into the stiff Huntington-Harrington territory. Harrison is one of today's baby name winners, ranking at Number 181, along with other popular patronymics.

As a surname, Harrison has both presidential and Beatle connections.

Harry

Diminutive of Henry, "estate ruler"
Harry was everyone's elderly uncle until Princess Diana, following British royal tradition, used Harry as a nickname for her son Henry. Then *Harry Potter* hit the charts and Harry Styles of the boy band One Direction became a pop star, leaving Harry's avuncular image in the dust. Harry is still much more popular in England (it was Number 1 for two years running), Ireland and Scotland than it is in the U.S. (Number 709), but its classic yet unpretentious image makes it a recommended choice.

Harry is the medieval English form of Henry, and was the nickname of all eight King Henrys; it is also a diminutive of Harold. Harry was a Top 20 name in this country from 1880 to 1918, and continued in the Top 100 into the 1950s (hence the song "I'm Just Wild About Harry"), and has countless worthy namesakes, including Truman, Belafonte and Houdini.

Among the celebs who have chosen this good-guy name for their sons are David Letterman (it was his father's name), Simon Baker and Billy Bob Thornton. And it's found in a number of movie titles from *The Trouble with Harry* to *Dirty Harry* to *When Harry Met Sally*.

Hart

English, "stag"

Hart could be the hero of a romantic novel, but on the other hand, it's short, straightforward, and strong sounding. The most famous bearer of the name was tragic poet Hart (born Harold) Crane, but it also has musical cred via Lorenz Hart, of the classic Rodgers & Hart songwriting duo and a literary tie to playwright Moss Hart.

Hart would make an interesting middle name choice — with heart.

Harvey

French, "battle worthy"

Hard as it may be for many American parents to believe, this Norman name is enjoying a big style revival in England — it's in the Top 50 there — along with similar choices like Stanley and Arthur. And it just could happen here, what with the many other "Har"-starting names trending for both girls and boys.

Harvey did have a respectable run as a Top 100 name in the US in the late nineteenth and early decades of the twentieth century, after which it began to get a bit of a nerdy rep.

Harvey, which was brought to England by the Normans and is a version of the French name Herve, does have some noteworthy references, such as a blind sixth-century saint who was said to be a monk and minstrel able to talk to animals. Later Harveys include industrialist Firestone, martyred San Francisco public figure Milk, comics legend Pekar, and performers Keitel, Korman and Fierstein, and movie producer Weinstein. Harvey was the name of an invisible man-sized rabbit who could only be seen by Jimmy Stewart's Elwood P. Dowd in a popular 1950 movie, and was the name of the main character in Rudyard Kipling's novel *Captains Courageous*.

Hawk

Nature name, "hawk, a bird"

Animal names are on the rise, especially more of the aggressive Hawk-Fox-Wolf variety than cute little Bunnys or Robins, and Hawk is a prime example.

Hawk is more commonly heard as a surname, represented by überskateboarder Tony Hawk, a pioneer of modern vertical skateboarding. Variations include Hawke, as in actor Ethan, Hawks, as in Golden Age movie director Howard, Hawking, as in scientist Stephen, and Hawkins, as in musicians Coleman, Screamin' Jay and Sophie B, and recently given to his baby boy by Tony Romo.

Hector

Greek, "holding fast"

Previously used primarily by Latino families, this name of the great hero of the Trojan War as related in Homer's *Iliad* is beginning to be considered more seriously by others seeking noble ancient hero names as well — it was also the name of the knight who raised King Arthur as his own son.

Currently ranking Number 267 — slightly down from its mid-1990s high, Hector is Number 31 in Spain, and popular in other Spanish-speaking countries, in France, and in Scotland where it is an Anglicization of Eachann.

In addition to being used for many contemporary Hispanic movie and TV characters, other Hectors appeared in such films as *Mystic Pizza* and *Lars and the Real Girl*. In literature, you can find Hectors in Thackeray's *Vanity Fair* and Balzac's *Cousin Bette*.

Some notable real-life Hectors: composer Berlioz and actor Elizando.

Hendrix

Dutch and German, from first name Hendrik

Hendrix is one of those hip rock and roll names, like Lennon, Jagger and Presley, that have been used by fellow celebs and others, to honor the seminal guitarist / singer / songwriter Jimi. And this one has the trendy "x" ending, as well.

Henry

German, "estate ruler"

Henry, after hovering around the latter half of the Top 100 for thirty-five years, is now at its highest point since 1956; its stylishness has increased substantially to the point where in upmarket neighborhoods and suburbs, it seems every other boy is named either Jack or Henry. Still, Henry is a solid name with lots of history and personality, and a favorite — it ranked Number 3 for recent searches — on Nameberry.

Henry has a long pedigree as a royal name with many worthy (as well as notorious) namesakes. There's Henry the Eighth, of course, along with all those other British kings named Henry, down to the current third in line to the throne, Prince Henry, called Harry. Other illustrious Henrys that might provide baby name inspiration include Henry David Thoreau, Henry (called Hank) Aaron, Henry James, Henry Ford, and Henry Miller.

Numerous celebs have chosen Henry for their sons, from Julia Roberts to Minnie Driver to Heidi Klum to Colin Farrell.

Appealing international versions include Arrigo, Enrico, Enzio, and Enrique.

Hiram

Hebrew, "brother of the exalted one"

Hiram is the kind of forgotten biblical name that adventurous parents who wish to move beyond David and Daniel are beginning to reconsider — even though it has bits of its old stiff-collared image clinging to it, along with a little hillbilly feel as well.

The name belonged to an Old Testament king of Tyre who helped David and Solomon plan and build the temple in Jerusalem, and was a favorite in the eighteenth and nineteenth centuries, though a couple of well-known bearers dropped it — Ulysses S. Grant was originally Hiram Ulysses Grant, but he didn't like having the initials H.U.G., and country singer Hank Williams was also born Hiram.

With its definite funk factor, and its friendly nickname Hi, Hiram would make a distinctive choice.

Holden

English, "hollow valley"

Holden is a classic case of a name that jumped out of a book and onto birth certificates — though it took quite a while. Parents who loved J. D. Salinger's *The Catcher in the Rye* are flocking to the name of its hero, Holden Caulfield — not coincidentally in tune with the Hudson-Hayden-Colton field of names. (Trivia note: Salinger supposedly came up with the name while looking at a movie poster promoting a film starring William Holden and Joan Caulfield, though other sources say he was named after Salinger's friend Holden Bowler.) Another impetus was provided by a soap opera character introduced in 1985.

Among the celebs who have chosen Holden are Brendan Fraser and Mira Sorvino.

Homer

Greek, "security, pledge"

Homer is a name that has traveled from the ancient Greek scribe of the great classical epics to Bart Simpson's doltish dad — and has also become the surprise hot celebrity pick of such parents as Richard Gere (his father's name), Bill Murray, and Anne Heche. *Simpsons* creator Matt Groening has both a father and a son named Homer.

Because of the epic scope of *The Odyssey* and *The Iliad*, the term "homeric" implies work on an enormous scale, while "homeric laughter" references the unrestrained laughter of the Greek gods.

With its quirky resume, Homer could make an interesting choice.

Horatio

English variation of Latin Horatius, "hour, time"

Like Horace, Horatio is a variation on the Latin Horatius, but its Shakespearean and optimistic Horatio Alger pedigree makes it an attractive up-and-comer, especially with its cool final o. A modern reference is the charismatic TV character Horatio Caine played by David Caruso in *CSI: Miami*.

Horatio was the given name of Lord Nelson, one of the most dashing of British heroes, the naval commander who led the British fleet to destroy the French at Trafalgar, and it also belonged to Hamlet's loyal friend. Another literary namesake is Captain Horatio Hornblower, the protagonist of a long-running series of naval novels penned by C. S. Forester, played on screen by Gregory Peck.

Hudson

English, "Hugh's son"; place name

Hudson has risen quickly up the charts after emerging at the bottom of the list in 1995, now at Number 93 and climbing.

Hudson has gotten a boost as a prominent surname over the years, from explorer Henry to heartthrob Rock to director Hugh, the musical Hudson brothers, and Kate Hudson today. It has also been attached to a few prominent starbabies, including the sons of Marcia Gay Hardin, Gena Lee Nolan, and Drew Lachey.

Hudson also benefits from the fashion value of New York, which boasts, of course, the Hudson River. It literally means "son of Hudd," which was a nickname for both Hugh and Richard in the Middle Ages. Streamlined spelling Hud was the name of the macho title character of an iconic Paul Newman film; John Mellencamp has a son named Hud.

James Barbour pulled a gender switch when he named his daughter Hudson in 2008.

Hugh

English from German, "mind, intellect"

Patrician to the core, Hugh was firmly in the Top 100 until 1903, but now is used very quietly, though still hanging in on the Top 1000.

Hugh has always been particularly prevalent among the Irish — there have been twenty Irish Saint Hughs, and it's traditionally associated with the O'Donnell clan. Hugh was an early immigrant to the New World, where there were two Hughs in the first English-speaking settlement in America. Hugh's biggest drawback is its sound, barely more than an exhaled breath. Actor Hugh Jackman adds a dash of the romantic hero — and other prominent Hughs include Hugh Laurie (born James Hugh), Hugh Grant, Hugh Dancy —

and Hugh Hefner, known to the world as Hef.

Hew and Huw are the distinctively — probably too distinctively — spelled Welsh forms.

Hugo

Latinized form of Hugh, "mind, intellect"

Hugo, the Latin form of Hugh, has more heft and energy than the original — and of course we love names that end (or begin, for that matter) with an "o." This one is especially appealing because it's backed up by lots of solid history and European style. Hugo has been sitting comfortably in the 300-500 range, but this well may change due to the charming 2011 Martin Scorsese 3D movie, based on the novel *The Invention of Hugo Cabret* and starring Asa Butterfield.

In the seventh *Harry Potter* novel, Ron and Hermione have a son named Hugo; real life contemporary Hugos include Hugo Chavez, longtime President of Venezuela, and the fashion world's Hugo Boss. In the past there was the distinguished Supreme Court Justice Hugo Black.

Hugo is currently enjoying mass popularity in several European countries — it's a Top 10 name in Spain, France and Sweden, and has long been stylish in the U.K.

Trivia tidbit: The annual awards for sci-fi writing are called the Hugos, honoring early genre writer Hugo Gernsback.

Humphrey

German, "peaceful warrior"

Humphrey is an old name that might have faded completely was it not for that Bogie flair. A royal name in Britain, where it's used somewhat more frequently, Humphrey might just have some life beyond Bogart here, especially with the recent interest in the names of Golden Age Hollywood stars.

Humphrey was brought to England by the Normans and was made famous by Duke Humphrey, the fifteenth-century Duke of Gloucester and youngest son of Henry IV, a noted patron of literature, who appears in Shakespeare's *Henry IV*. In other literature, Humphrey Wasp is a character in Ben Jonson's *Bartholomew Fair*, and the eponymous hero of Tobias Smollett's early novel *Humphrey Clinker*.

Bottom line: An interesting name with a noirish edge.

Huxley

English, "inhospitable place"

Huxley is definitely rising as a surname name, with its "x" that makes almost any name cooler. Huxley honors writer Aldous, author of *Brave New World*, and other members of his distinguished family — and nickname Hux is nearly as adorable as Huck.

I

Ian

Scottish version of John, "the Lord is gracious"

Ian was introduced to Americans by Ian Fleming, creator of James Bond, and it's been on a steady path in the Top 100 ever since, due to its jaunty charm. Today, Ian flies in formation with fellow classic British RAF pilot names, like Derek and Miles and Colin, all now certified U.S. citizens, packing considerable punch and panache into its three short letters. So though it may not be the newest name on the block, it's still a recommended choice.

Notable namesakes include actor Ian McKellan and novelist Ian McEwan.

Ignatius

Latin, "fiery"

Ignatius? Good gracious! This is a name making a truly surprising return, sparked by its selection by not one but two celebrities — Cate Blanchett and Julianne Nicholson.

Ignatius, the name of several saints including the founder of the Catholic Jesuit order, was considered more apt to be borne by churches and schools than babies in the recent past, though it was not unusual from the late nineteenth century to 1930; it ranked as high as Number 602 in 1913.

The nickname Iggy definitely brings Ignatius down to earth. But if you find Ignatius appealing yet can't quite go all the way, you might want to consider Inigo.

Ignatius is the middle name of Percy Weasley in the *Harry Potter* books, and is a major character in John Kennedy Toole's *A Confederacy of Dunces*.

Indigo

Greek, "Indian dye"

Indigo is one of the most appealing and evocative of the new generation of color names. Color names have joined flower and jewel appellations — in a big way — and Indigo, a deep blue-purple dye from plants native to India, is particularly striking for both girls and boys. Indigo is the name of a character in the Ntozake Shange novel *Sassafrass, Cypress & Indigo*, and was used for his daughter by Lou Diamond Phillips.

Some cultural references: The Indigo Girls are a folk duo, *Mood Indigo* is a classic Duke Ellington jazz composition, and there is a 1970s New Age theory that Indigo children possess special, sometimes supernatural abilities.

Indio

Spanish, "Indian"

This name of a California desert town, used by Deborah Falconer and Robert Downey, Jr for their son, makes a much livelier and more individual — not to mention more masculine — improvisation on the themes of India and Indiana.

The similar sounding color name Indigo is unisex, but tending more to the girls — it was used by Lou Diamond Phillips for his daughter, as well as the group The Indigo Girls, but its "o" ending makes it boy-friendly too.

Inigo

Basque, medieval Spanish variation of Ignatius, "fiery"

Inigo, almost unknown in the U.S., is an intriguing choice, with its strong beat, creative and evocative sound, and associations with the great early British architect and stage designer Inigo Jones. The sixteenth / seventeenth-century Jones shared his name with his father, a London clockmaker, who received it when Spanish names were fashionable in England, especially among devout Roman Catholics.

Inigo Montoya is a character in *The Princess Bride*, played by Mandy Patinkin.

The pronunciation is with short "i"s and a hard "g": IN-ih-go.

Innes

Scottish, "from the river island"

Innis is the name of an island (and Gaelic word for island) which became a Scottish surname and clan name before being used as a first. It hasn't been heard much in the U.S., but could attract more attention with the growing popularity of Latin "s"-ending boys' names such as Atticus.

Innis is related in sound to Ennis, as in the character name Ennis Del Mar, indelibly played by Heath Ledger in *Brokeback Mountain*.

Isaac

Hebrew, "laughter"

Isaac has shaved off his biblical beard and leaped into the Top 30, where it's been for the past few years — outrunning cousin Isaiah — and showing signs of heading even higher. A favorite of the Puritans, Isaac went on to assume something of a rabbinical image. In the Old Testament, Isaac was the long-awaited son of the elderly Sarah and 100-year-old Abraham, so old that their news provoked laughter, giving the name its meaning.

A baby given this name can point to many distinguished namesakes, including Isaacs (and Izaaks) Newton, Walton, Bashevis Singer, Asimov, Stern and Hayes. The name was somewhat rejuvenated by onetime heartthrob Isaac Hanson.

Isaac also boasts the cute nicknames of Izzy — now shared, however, with a bevy of Isabellas — and Ike.

Isaiah

Hebrew, "Salvation of the Lord"
Isaiah, like brethren Isaac and Elijah, is a once neglected biblical name now firmly back in favor, already surpassing such long-popular Old Testament stalwarts as Aaron and Adam.

The biblical Isaiah, son of Amos, was the most important of the major prophets, with an Old Testament book named for him.

Isaiah has been a star player on the contemporary athletic field, with several prominent basketball and football player namesakes, in addition to a memorable character on *Little House on the Prairie,* and *Grey's Anatomy* actor Isaiah Washington.

Beyond that, two sports figures have named their sons Isaiah: Allen Iverson and Tim (and wife Elisabeth) Hasselbeck. Basketball superstar Isiah Thomas helped popularize that streamlined spelling of the name.

Ishmael

Hebrew, "God will hearken"; Arabic, "outcast"
Ishmael is most familiar through "Call me Ishmael," the opening line spoken by the youthful narrator of *Moby-Dick.* Few American parents have followed that advice, though the Spanish and Arabic spelling, Ismael, ranks at Number 362. But with its warm and pleasant sound, we could see Ishmael tagging along behind Isaiah and Isaac.

In the Bible, Ishmael was Abraham's first son by the Egyptian maidservant Hagar, who was told by God to name him Ishmael. In Islamic tradition, Ishmael (or Ismail) is believed to have been the ancestor of the Arabs.

Ishmael Bush is one of the main characters in James Fenimore Cooper's novel *The Prairie,* and there is an Ismael in the Lemony Snicket book, *The End.* Some notable real-life bearers are novelist and poet Ishmael Reed and Indian-born film producer Ismail Merchant.

Isidore

Greek, "gift of Isis"

Isabel and Isadora are back: could it now be time for a more widespread revival of Isidore?

A common ancient Greek name belonging to several saints — including Saint Isidore the Ploughman, patron saint of Madrid and the great encyclopedist St. Isidore of Seville, whose work formed the basis of much medieval knowledge — Isidore was adopted by Spanish Jews to the point where it was almost their exclusive property.

In addition to the obvious Izzy, another traditional nickname is Dore/Dory.

Ivor

Scottish variation of Welsh Ifor, "lord" or English form of Scandinavian Ifar, "yew"
Ivor, a favorite choice for upscale characters in Brit Lit novels by authors like P.G. Wodehouse and Evelyn Waugh, is an interesting and unusual name just waiting to be discovered by parents in this country.

Ivor Novello was the stage name of a popular Welsh actor and songwriter of the recent past who brought it to prominence in England.

An equally appealing name is the related Ivo, which has the energetic impact of all names ending in "o."

J

Jabez

Hebrew, "borne in pain"

Jabez has a rare combo of three appealing elements: a biblical heritage, a captivating Southern accent, and a jazzy feel. It was popular with the Pilgrims and on into the nineteenth century (there have been four U.S. Congressmen named Jabez), but it hasn't been in the Top 1000 since 1880.

Jabez came back into the spotlight in 2000 with the publication of Bruce Wilkinson's book *The Prayer of Jabez*, based on the Old Testament passage beginning "Jabez was more honorable than his brothers." The book became an international hit selling nine million copies and heading the New York Times bestseller list.

In literature, Jabez Stone was the main character in the story and film *The Devil and Daniel Webster*, and a principal character in a Sherlock Holmes story. Real life Jabezes include a founding partner of Standard Oil.

Jack

English, diminutive of John, "God is gracious"

Jack was, until 2011 when he was unseated by Oliver, for years the Number 1 name in England and is firmly in the Top 50 here, having returned to the Top 100 in 1996. Jack is a durable, cheery everyman form of John, and has been chosen for their sons by dozens of celebs, such as Matt Lauer, Luke Perry, Meg Ryan and Kirk Cameron.

How did John get to Jack? It went from John to Johnkin to Jankin to Jackin to Jack.

Familiar to all from earliest childhood via Jack and Jill, Jack Sprat, Jack and the Beanstalk and Little Jack Horner et al, the name was so common in the Middle Ages that Jack became a generic term for a man.

Jack is still a favorite for recent novel, TV and movie characters, including *24*'s Jack Bauer, *Lost*'s Jack Shepard and *30 Rock*'s Jack Donaghy. Dads especially seem to like Jack.

Internationally, in addition to Britain, Jack has been a top name in Scotland, Northern Ireland, Australia and New Zealand for well over a decade.

The jaunty Scottish version is Jock.

Jackson

English, "son of Jack"

Cool name Jackson is one of the celebrisphere's top favorites, having been chosen by, among others, Spike Lee, Poppy Montgomery, Carson Daly, Maria Bello, Natalie Maines, Scott Wolf, Maya Rudolph, and Katey Sagal. After a spectacular rise, this stylish presidential name has been in the Top 25 since 2010.

In addition to historic namesakes Andrew and Stonewall, some art-loving parents may wish to honor Abstract Expressionist painter Jackson Pollock.

Jackson is so popular that it now ranks higher on the Social Security list than either John or Jack, perhaps because parents see it as more modern than John and a fuller name than Jack.

Following in its wake are the streamlined spellings Jaxon and Jaxson, which are also increasing in popularity.

Jagger

English occupational name, "carter"

Jagger is a swaggering Rolling Stone of a name that's been picked up by a number of fellow celebs, including Lindsay Davenport and Brett Scallions — while Soleil Moon Frye pulled a gender switch when she bestowed it on her daughter. It's edgy with a touch of danger.

Pamela Anderson and Tommy Lee started the ball rolling when they gave their son Dylan the middle name of Jagger in 1997; it entered the popularity list in 2001.

James

English variation of Jacob, Hebrew, "supplanter"

James is one of the classic Anglo-Saxon names, a stalwart through the ages, which is more popular and — yes — stylish than ever today. It recently came out Number 1 in a poll of America's favorite boys' baby names.

James is biblical (the name of two apostles in the New Testament), royal (kings of both England and Scotland), presidential (with more U.S. Chief Executives named James [6] than any other name), and it is shared by countless great writers and entertainers. James is still in the Top 20 and a current favorite among fashionable parents looking for a baby name that has both style and substance.

There are fewer Jimmys, Jimbos or even Jamies these days: the most fashionable form of the name is James itself. Several stylish celebrities have chosen it in recent years for their sons, including Sarah Jessica Parker and Matthew Broderick, Liz Phair, Colin Farrell and Isaac Hanson, while Brendan Fehr thought out of the box and named his daughter James.

James has some interesting foreign variations: Diego and Jaime (Spanish), Jacques (French), Giacomo (Italian), Hamish (Scottish), Jaako (Finnish), Seamus (Irish), Jaap (Dutch) and Jago (Cornish).

Jared

Hebrew, "he descends"

Jared is an Old Testament name that has been popular for decades — it was revived in the 60s via TV westerns — and is still an appealing option.

In the Bible, Jared was a descendant of Adam who became the father of Enoch at the age of 162 — and then lived on for another eight hundred years. Two contemporary Jareds are actors Jared Leto and Jared Harris. Jared Cameron is a shape-shifting werewolf character in the *Twilight* series of books and movies.

Other spellings include Jarred, Jarrad, Jarrod and Jarod.

Jarvis

English variation of Gervase, meaning unknown

Jarvis, one of the original two-syllable nouveau boys' choices, is a saint's name with a certain retro charm and a nice quirky feel. Though Jarvis peaked in the late 1880s, he is beginning to sound fresh again.

Jarvis Lorry is a character in Dickens's *A Tale of Two Cities*, and there was another Jarvis in Upton Sinclair's *The Jungle*. Probably the best known modern Jarvis is British rocker Jarvis Cocker.

Jasper

Persian, "bringer of treasure"

Jasper has a lot going for it — in the past years it shot up 112 places and is still rising, after long being considered a hip and charming name in England. Distinctly masculine, Jasper represents a variety of quartz — one of the few gem names for boys — and is the first name of the great modern artist Jasper Johns. Our only caveat: Jasper is a favorite of a lot of hip parents, and will also be picked up through its strong appearance in the *Twilight* books and movies.

Jasper is the usual English form for one of the three Wise Men who brought gifts to the infant Christ according to medieval tradition, and appears in the Bible as a reference to the stone itself in Revelations 4:3.

Jasper has considerable literary cred as well, appearing in works by Sir Walter Scott, James Fenimore Cooper, Thackeray, and Thomas Hardy — as well as Stephenie Meyer.

Casper/Caspar is the German version.

Jax

Modern invented name

Jax is the Dex-Jex-Bix type of "x" ending cool — possibly too cool — variation of Jack or nickname for Jaxon or Jackson. Jax has shot up almost 400 places in the last four years and is one of the fastest-rising boys' names.

Jax was a soap opera character name way back when; most recently he's been seen as Jackson "Jax" Teller, the central character on *Sons of Anarchy*, the national president of the Sons of Anarchy Motorcycle Club.

Jeb

Diminutive of Jebediah, Hebrew, "beloved friend"

Both Jeb and Jed are very attractive Old Testament short forms with long and bright futures. Jeb's main current association is with the Bush brother and former governor of Florida, but the name was a mainstay on early TV westerns, and then went upscale as the nickname (his birth name being Josiah) of the President on *The West Wing*.

Jebediah Obadiah Zachariah Jedediah Springfield was the fictitious founder of the Simpsons's hometown. As for Civil War Confederate General Jeb Stuart, his nickname sprang from his initials — his full name was James Ewell Brown.

Jedidiah

Hebrew, "beloved of the Lord"

Jedidiah, an Old Testament name with a touch of Gunsmoke-era western panache, is right in line to be revived along with the other biblical "iah" names; it's currently in the Top 900.

Jedidiah was the name given by the prophet Nathan to King Solomon in the Old Testament. An inspiration to hiking enthusiasts might be the intrepid explorer and trailblazer Jedidiah Strong Smith.

Jed is the inevitable nickname.

Jefferson

English, "son of Jeffrey"

The name of the third U.S. President sounds, like Harrison and Jackson, more modern and stylish now than its root name. Used as a first name long before our surname-crazed era, Jefferson was most famously connected to the President of the Confederacy, Jefferson Davis — and is the middle name of another Prez, William Clinton. Then there are Jefferson Bricks in Dickens's *Martin Chuzzlewit* and Jefferson Almond in Henry James's *Washington Square*, and Jefferson Smith, the title character in the Frank Capra classic film *Mr. Smith Goes to Washington*, plus others — for better and for worse — in *Married With Children*, *The Dukes of Hazzard*, and *Kit Kittridge: An American Girl*.

Admittedly, nickname Jeff does sound a bit dated.

Jenson

Scandinavian, "son of Jens"
The surname name Jenson is in the British Top 100 thanks to champion race car driver Jenson Button. Jenson might be an honorific for an ancestral John, the English form of Jens or Johannes, or even Jen. Jensen is an alternate spelling.

Jeremiah

Hebrew, "appointed by God"
Jeremiah, which is now just outside the Top 50 — is a solid Old Testament prophet name that has gradually taken the place of the now dated Jeremy, Gerard and Gerald, joining other currently popular biblical "iah" names like Josiah and Isaiah. In the Bible Jeremiah is a famous prophet whose story is recorded in the book named after him.

Dickens used the name in two of his novels — *Little Dorrit* and *A Tale of Two Cities* — and other fictional Jeremiahs have been spotted in such movies and TV shows as *Oz*, *Zoey 101* and *The Princess Diaries*. Leonard Bernstein composed a work called Jeremiah Symphony.

Caveats: Once-logical nickname Jerry sounds like the family dentist, and some may make the Jeremiah bullfrog association.

A related, more unusual biblical option: Jeriah.

Jericho

Biblical place-name
A biblical place name with trumpeting verve and strength.

Though rarely heard as a first name, Jericho has appeared in the titles of films, TV series, songs, bands, comics, and video games (Clive Barker's *Jericho*).

Jethro

Hebrew, "abundance" or "excellence"
Jethro, though the biblical father-in-law of Moses, has suffered for a long time from a

Beverly Hillbilly image, but some really adventurous parents might consider updating and urbanizing it and transitioning it into the hip "o" ending category.

The 60s rock group Jethro Tull was named for an eighteenth-century British agricultural reformer and inventor.

Joaquin

Spanish variation of Joachim, "God will judge"

Actor Joaquin Phoenix (brother of River, Rain, Liberty and Summer) highlighted this one, then Kelly Ripa began talking about younger son Joaquin on her daily TV show, and presto — it's now one of the hottest and most appealing multicultural choices, ranking at Number 325.

Joaquin is currently enjoying high popularity in South America — it's in the Top 6 in both Argentina and Chile.

Colorful poet Joaquin (born Cincinnatus) Miller was known as the "Byron of the Rockies." There is a teenage character in Hemingway's *For Whom the Bell Tolls* named Joaquin; and San Joaquín is the Spanish version of Saint Joachim, the traditional name for the father of Mary, mother of Jesus.

Joe

Diminutive of Joseph, "Jehovah increases"

Joe is still the ultimate good-guy name, not at all diminished by its longevity or popularity or its everyman rep as Regular Joe, Cowboy Joe, G.I. Joe, Joe Millionaire, Joe Blow, or even Average Joe.

There are millions of Josephs who have gone primarily by the nickname Joe; just a few of the more prominent are Joes Biden, Namath, Torre, DiMaggio, Lieberman, Montana and Jonas.

Several celebrities have chosen Joe as a full name for their sons, including Kate Winslet, Kevin Costner, Sting and Stephen King — or you could start with recommended choices Joseph, Josiah, or Jonah and end up at Joe.

Jonah

Hebrew, "dove"

Jonah, the name of the Old Testament prophet who was swallowed by the whale, only to emerge unharmed three days later, is increasingly appreciated by parents looking for a biblical name less common than Jacob or Joshua, yet not too obscure — it's now at Number 131. Plus, Jonah comes with a ready-made nursery-decorating motif.

The appealing Jonah has been featured in such movies as *Sleepless in Seattle* and *Knocked Up*, and is currently represented by actor/writer Jonah Hill.

Jonas is the Greek version.

Jonas

Greek variation of Jonah, "dove"

Jonas has a slightly more grandfatherly image than the English version of his name, but that only adds to its retro appeal. And though it may lag behind Jonah in this country, Jonas is riding a huge wave of popularity in Europe, where it ranks highly in Germany, Switzerland, Austria and Norway — where it was the top name for several recent years.

Over time, Jonas has been associated with Dr. Jonas Salk, developer of the anti-polio vaccine and tween fave group the Jonas Brothers. Charles Dickens used the name for a character in *Martin Chuzzlewit*.

Joseph

Hebrew, "Jehovah increases"

Joseph is one of the most classic names in American nomenclature, popular with parents from many ethnic backgrounds and having dual-religious appeal. In the Old Testament, Joseph is the twelfth and favorite son of Jacob and Rachel; in the New Testament it is the name of the carpenter husband of the Virgin Mary, mother of Christ.

Even if Joseph may be dipping slightly in the popularity charts, it will always be a strong and solid choice. Variations of Joseph are popular worldwide, including Jose, Giuseppe, and Josef, while the female Josephine is a currently enjoying a style revival. Almost everyone has a Joseph in their family tree, and Joe is an always-winning nickname.

Josiah

Hebrew, "God supports, heals"

Josiah — a biblical name with lots of quaint, old-fashioned charm — makes a much fresher sounding alternative to either Joseph or Joshua, combining the best of both. Josiah is now at Number 79.

In the Old Testament, Josiah was an upright king of Judah; two Josiahs, Wedgwood and Spode, founded the fine English potteries that bear their names. Josiah Bartlett was a signer of the Declaration of Independence, and the President on *The West Wing* shared his name, being a fictional descendant.

Charles Dickens used the name for a character in his novel *Hard Times* and Josiah Borden is a character in Eugene O'Neill's tragedy *Mourning Becomes Electra*.

Jubal

Latin, "joyous celebration"; Hebrew, "ram's horn"

This unusual name might be a possibility for musical families: Jubal was credited in Genesis with the invention of the lyre, flute, harp, and organ. It also has a jubilant feel through its sound and meaning, and has had some southern popularity via Confederate general Jubal Anderson Early. George Eliot wrote a poem called *The Legend of Jubal*.

There have been a few Jubals in contemporary culture as well: Jubal Harshaw in Robert A. Heinlein's sci-fi classic *Stranger in a Strange Land* and Jubal Early in Joss Whedon's TV cult favorite, *Firefly*.

Judah

Hebrew, "praised"

Judah is the strong, resonant Old Testament name of the son of Jacob who was the ancestor of one of the tribes of Israel, and from whom the word Jew is derived. Some of the name's newfound popularity might be attributable to the similarly named Jude Law. In 2012, Judah had risen more than seven hundred spots since 1998 — so definitely one of the biblical boys names moving up!

Judah Maccabee is acclaimed as one of the greatest warriors in Jewish history. In popular culture, Judah Ben-Hur was the eponymous hero of the novel and film, *Ben-Hur*, and, more recently, is borne by Judah Friedlander of *30 Rock*, and is the name of the young son of Lucy Lawless.

Judd

Medieval short form of Jordan, "flowing down"

Judd is a strong but sensitive short form that can easily stand on its own, the second "d" giving it a lot more substance, and it would also be a good middle name choice. Two recent actors have given it credence — Judd Nelson and Judd Hirsch, and now it's most noticeably represented by comedy director Judd Apatow.

Judd is a fairly prevalent surname, represented by the family of Naomi, Wynonna and Ashley, and the minimalist artist Donald Judd.

Jude

Latin diminutive of Judah, "praised"

Jude is an example of a name whose image was turned on its head primarily by one appealing celebrity. So take a bow, Jude Law: You — in collaboration with the Lennon-McCartney song "Hey Jude" — have erased Jude's old connections to the traitorous Judas Iscariot and Thomas Hardy's tragic *Jude the Obscure*, and inspired a legion of new babies named Jude — over two thousand of them last year.

Saint Jude was the apostle who interceded for people with problems and became the patron saint of lost causes.

Kelsey Grammer has a son named Jude Gordon. Jude is occasionally used for girls (as in Martha Stewart's granddaughter) — but more often as a shortened form of Judith/Judy.

Jules

French form of Latin Julius, "youthful, downy"

Though Jules hasn't been on the US popularity list in fifty years, it is a current hit in its native France — where it's now Number 6 — and we can definitely see it making a comeback here, being far more romantic than, say, Jim.

The glittering Jules has a solid history, attached to such cultural notables as author Verne, opera composer Massenet, painter Olitski and cartoonist Feiffer, as well as appearing as a character in such iconic films as *Pulp Fiction* and *St. Elmo's Fire*, and in Balzac's novel *The Human Comedy* and Ayn Rand's *Atlas Shrugged*. These days, Jules is also apt to be heard as a nickname for the feminine Julia or Julie, as in TV personality Jules Asner, the Keira Knightley character in *Bend it Like Beckham*, and celebrity chef Jamie Oliver's wife — spelled Jools. Jools is, in fact, a more modern, hip spelling.

Julian

English from Latin, variation of Julius, "youthful, downy"

Julian is a rising star, having overcome the somewhat pale, aesthetic image it projected in the past and become a solid, handsome, recommended choice.

Julian has numerous historic and cultural references. In addition to St Julian the Hospitaller, patron saint of travelers, and the Roman emperor Julian, there are activist/politician Julian Bond, singer Julian Lennon, novelist Julian Barnes and painter/filmmaker Julian Schnabel, as well as the hero of Stendhal's *The Red and the Black* and characters on such TV shows as *Alias* and *Law & Order*.

In addition to its being just outside the Top 50 in the US, Julian has been enjoying an international resurgence in recent years, at Number 8 in Austria, and in the Top 20 in Germany, the Netherlands, Malta, Switzerland, and Brazil.

Celebrities who have chosen Julian for their sons include Robert De Niro, Lisa Kudrow, Jerry Seinfeld, and Paula Patton and Robin Thicke.

Jolyon is an interesting variant form, Julien is the French spelling, and Giuliano is the attractive Italian version.

Julius

Latin, "youthful, downy"

Immortal through its association with the ancient Caesar (it was his clan name), Julius may still lag behind Julian, but is definitely starting to make a comeback, and in fact feels more cutting edge, in line with the current trend for Latin "ius" ending names.

A common Christian name in Roman times — as in Pope Julius I — it was rarely used in English-speaking countries until the nineteenth century. Some Julius connections: basketball great Julius Erving — Dr. J, characters in the *Artemis Fowl* series and *Everybody Hates Chris* (as Dad), Groucho Marx's birth name, the comic monkey created by Paul Frank, and the Orange Julius drink.

Jupiter

Roman mythology name

Jupiter's partner Juno has entered the mainstream, so it's possible that her divine mate could follow. The name of the supreme Roman deity and the largest planet has until recently had either too hippie or too grandiose a feel for most mortals, but with the rise of sound-alike Juniper and space names such as Orion and Mars, Jupiter may find new favor.

Short form Jupe is adorable.

Justice and Justus

Word name

Justice, one of the rare virtue names for boys, entered the popularity ranks in 1992, and has remained on the list ever since. Parents search for names implying virtue has led to a mini-revival of this long-neglected name in both its German homonymic form, Justus, and as the word itself. Steven Seagal was ahead of the curve when he used it back in 1976.

With the Justus spelling, it was the name of several saints and noted scholars and scientists.

Caveat: Justice is now being used for girls almost as frequently as for boys.

K

Kai

Hawaiian, "sea"

Kai is a strong, evocative, exotic multi-cultural name — meaning "sea" in Hawaiian, "forgiveness" in Japanese, "willow tree" in Navajo, and "earth" in Scandinavian — that packs a lot of power in its single syllable.

Famous as the boy enchanted by the fairy-tale *Snow Queen,* Kai was chosen for her son by actress Jennifer Connelly and as a middle name for son Samuel by Naomi Watts and Liev Schreiber. Kai is popular with Nameberries as both a first and middle name choice. Its most prominent namesake is Danish-born jazz trombonist Kai Winding, and it is popular in computer games.

Kai is currently in the Top 200 in the U.S., and in the Top 70 in Britain, Scotland, Canada and Australia — and as high as Number 5 on the island of Malta.

Kai is occasionally given to girls; Donald Trump, Jr has a daughter named Kai Madison.

Keaton

English, "shed town"

Keaton is an engaging surname with warmth, energy, and a sense of humor, identified with silent comedian Buster Keaton and contemporary actress Diane Keaton. Although rare as a first name, a young Keaton would fit right in with classmates Keenan and Kellen.

Keegan

Irish, "son of Egan"

Keegan is one of a clan of spirited Irish surnames starting with "K" and ending with "n" — this one with the cheery double "e" in the middle — that are appealing to an increasing number of parents. It derives from Mac Aodhagáin, meaning "son (or descendant) of Aodhagán," a diminutive of the Irish name Aodh — pronounced Aye.

The related name Egan is another recommended possibility.

Kenyon

English, "white haired or blond"

Kenyon is a very engaging British surname name, the middle *y* giving it a kind of southwestern canyonesque undertone.

Though Kenyon appears in English records as far back as the fourteenth century and arrived in America in the seventeenth, it sounds cooler these days than the more traditional Kenneth.

Kenyon has literary ties to the prestigious journal The Kenyon Review, originating from Ohio's Kenyon College, and sports enthusiasts will recognize it as the name of basketball star Kenyon Martin (nicknamed K-Mart), who plays for the LA Clippers.

Kenzo

Japanese, "strong and healthy"

Kenzo is a common Japanese name with several creative bearers: the single-named fashion designer, prizewinning architect Kenzo Takada, and painter Kenzo Okada, which makes it internationally recognizable.

Kenzo was chosen for their son by Kimora Lee Simmons and Djimon Hounsou, inspired by the designer.

Kenzo can have other meanings, all positive, depending on the Japanese characters used.

Kermit

Irish, variant of Diarmaid/Dermot, "free man"

Kermit was a Top 500 name until the 1960s, not coincidentally the decade in which Kermit the Frog became well known, proving that it isn't easy being green, even for a name. But we think it's time for some of those appealing *Sesame Street* names — Kermit, Elmo, Grover — to be taken out of that context and be considered on their own.

Historically, Kermit is known via Kermit Roosevelt, soldier and explorer son of President Theodore Roosevelt.

And if you're still not convinced, you can consider Dermot.

Kiefer

German, "barrel maker"

Kiefer is a strong occupational surname associated with *24* star Kiefer Sutherland, but one that could well join the other "er" surnames currently in favor.

Kiefer Sutherland, the son of actor Donald Sutherland, was named for director Warren Kiefer, who gave Donald Sutherland his first movie role. Donald was a firm believer in honoring valued friends and mentors — his other sons are named Roeg, Rossif and Angus. Kiefer Sutherland's full name is Kiefer William Frederick Dempsey George Rufus.

Another possible cultural namesake is the esteemed German artist Anselm Kiefer.

Kieran

Irish, "little dark one"

Long popular in Ireland and England, Kieran, the name of Ireland's first-born saint and twenty-five other saints, has been building its U.S. fan base. Strong and attractive, with a fashionable Irish brogue, its only drawback is possible confusion with such female choices as Karen and Kyra. While Ciaran is the more authentic Irish spelling, the anglicized Kieran will be easier for Americans to understand.

Julianna Margulies chose Kieran for her son, and Kieran is a Culkin brother to Macaulay and Rory. Kier is an attractive short form, and Kiera/Keira is Kieran's girl twin.

Killian

Irish, "war, strife"

This Irish classic, most commonly spelled Killian in the U.S. and Cillian in its native land, is one of several newer recommended Gaelic choices that have entered the American name pool. Killian now stands at Number 756 in the American polls, while Cillian is 22 in its Irish homeland.

There are several Saint Cillians, including one who was sent to Bavaria to convert the natives and was martyred for his trouble. The best known contemporary bearer of the name in versatile actor Cillian Murphy.

Kingston

English, "king's town"

Chosen for their first son by musical couple Gwen Stefani and Gavin Rossdale, this Jamaican place and elegant British surname also boasts the more regal yet user-friendly short form, King.

Kingston offers clear evidence of the starbaby effect: it arrived on the popularity list at Number 937 in 2006, the year little Kingston Rossdale was born, and since has leaped more than 700 spots.

Knox

Scottish, "round hill"

Knox is an old Scottish surname that Brad Pitt (whose great-great-grandfather was named Hal Knox Hillhouse) and Angelina Jolie took out of the back cupboard, dusted off, and elevated to coolness — to the point where it entered the Social Security list's Top 1000 in 2009.

With Knox, the Jolie-Pitts established their own tradition: instead of their sons bearing the same first initial, they share the final letter "x" — Maddox, Pax and Knox — as well as a final "n" for their middle names.

Knox is a strong name that has already begun being adopted by other parents, following in the footsteps of brother Maddox — in just a few years it has moved to the Top 500 on the Most Popular list.

The surname Knox dates back at least to the thirteenth century and John Knox was the priest who brought about the Reformation in Scotland.

L

Lachlan

Scottish, "from the fjord-land"

Lachlan is as Scottish as haggis and tartan plaid kilts, a favorite used throughout England, Scotland, Australia and New Zealand — and just beginning to be noticed in the US. An ancient name, Lachlan was originally used to describe the Viking invaders of Scotland, those from the land of the lochs.

In Ireland, the name was Anglicized as Laughlin; in Scotland the pet forms are Lach, Lachie or Lockie.

Lachlan has been a top name in Australia for at least a decade and is currently Number 3 there. It has been in the headlines recently via the eldest son of media mogul Rupert Murdoch.

Somewhat surprisingly, Lachlan has US presidential cred, as the son of tenth president John Tyler, whose other children included a Lyon, a Letitia, a Tazewell and a Pearl.

Laird

Scottish, "lord of the land"

Laird is a Scottish title for the landed gentry — it ranks just below a Baron — with a pleasantly distinctive Scottish burr that must have appealed to Sharon Stone, who chose it for her son.

Laird Cregar was an early movie actor, known for playing creepy roles; Laird Hamilton is a famous American big-wave surfer.

Langston

English, "tall man's town"

The great African-American Harlem Renaissance writer Langston Hughes put this one on the map; actor Laurence Fishburne adopted it for his now-grown son, born in 1987.

Hughes was born James Mercer Langston Hughes, Langston being his mother's maiden name.

Some similar choices are Lanford, Landon, Langford and Langley.

Laredo

Place-name

We've seen babies with Texas city names like Austin, Houston and Dallas — why not the unexplored Laredo, which has a lot of cowboy charisma? Laredo might make for a more modern and creative namesake for an Uncle Lawrence/Larry — as could the related Laramie.

There was a 1960s TV Western series about the Texas Rangers titled *Laredo*. There is also a famous cowboy ballad, *Streets of Laredo*, recorded by Johnny Cash, and a Band of Horses song called simply *Laredo*.

Lars

Scandinavian from Latin Laurentius, "crowned with laurel"

Lars is a perfect candidate for a cross-cultural passport: it has been heard often enough here to sound familiar and friendly, yet retains the charisma of a charming foreigner.

In this country Lars has been particularly associated with two Danes — Metallica's Lars Ulrich and film director Lars von Trier. In the 2007 movie *Lars and the Real Girl*, protagonist Lars Lindstrom was played by Ryan Gosling.

Laszlo

Hungarian, "glorious ruler"

The Hungarian classic Laszlo, with its zippy "z" middle and energetic "o" ending, has become something of a hipster option, beginning to be considered by cutting-edge parents.

A name with a royal heritage in its native country in the Ladislaus form, it is still in the Hungarian Top 20.

Laszlo is probably most familiar to Americans via the noble Paul Henreid character in *Casablanca*, who was Czech; there have been other fictional Laszlos in *Real Genius* and the *Doctor Who* series, and Laszlo is the name of the Ralph Fiennes character in *The English Patient*.

Real life namesakes include painter Moholy-Nagy and acclaimed cinematographer Kovacs. Two well-known actors who were born with the name Laszlo are Peter Lorre and Leslie Howard.

The spelling of the name can be streamlined to Lazlo.

Lazarus

Greek variation of Hebrew Eleazar, "God is my helper"

Lazarus is a name that looks as if it could possibly be raised from the dead, just like its biblical bearer. Look for it in the next wave of Old Testament revivals that transcend their long-bearded images, the way Noah, Moses, and Abraham have for this generation.

In the Bible, there are two people named Lazarus, the better known being the brother of Mary and Martha of Bethany whom Jesus raised from the dead. There have been also several saints named Lazarus.

As a surname, Lazarus is most identified with poet Emma Lazarus, whose words are displayed on the Statue of Liberty.

Related options are the original Hebrew Eleazar, the Italian and Spanish Lazaro, and the Yiddish form Lazer/Laser, the name of the son in the film *The Kids are All Right*.

Leander

Greek, "lion-man"

Leander is an almost unknown name with great potential as a possible alternative to the overused Alexander. In Greek legend, Leander was the powerful figure who swam across the Hellespont every night to visit his beloved Hero, a priestess of Venus.

Leander is currently a Top 40 name in Norway; Leandro is the attractive Spanish form, and Leandre is popular in France — it appears in three Molière plays.

Leander Sydnor was the name of one of the younger police detectives on *The Wire*.

Leif

Scandinavian, "heir, descendant"

Leif is one of the most recognizable Scandinavian names, thanks to Icelandic explorer Leif Erikson, and is still one of the best, with a pleasant aural association with the word leaf.

Leif Erikson, son of explorer Eric the Red, was the first European to land in North America — some five hundred years before Columbus. Centuries later, the name became associated in the U.S. with 1970s teen idol Leif Garrett, the name peaking on the charts at Number 654 in 1970, dropping off completely in 1987.

Pronounced LAYF in its Scandinavian milieu, Lief is often pronounced as Leaf in this country. Joaquin Phoenix was for a time known as Leaf, in keeping with the nature names of his siblings.

Lemuel

Hebrew, "devoted to God"

Lemuel is a neglected Old Testament name, with the friendly nickname Lem, that we're surprised hasn't been picked up on by parents who have known too many Samuels.

In the Bible, Lemuel is mentioned twice in Proverbs as a king, but the name is probably remembered more as the first name of the narrator who journeys to Lilliput in Jonathan Swift's satirical *Gulliver's Travels*.

Lennon

Irish, "small cloak or cape"

A growing number of high-profile (and other) parents are choosing to honor their musical idols, such as Hendrix, Presley, Jagger, and now Lennon. Lennon first came to notice when Liam Gallagher and Patsy Kensit used it for their son in 1999, and singer-musician Adam Pascal followed their lead two years later.

Lennon made it onto the popularity list in 2008, edging up slightly every year since, though still given to only a couple of hundred boys annually.

In addition to its obvious Beatles connection, Lennon has a nice lemony feel.

Lennox

Scottish, "elm grove"

Lennox is an aristocratic and powerful Scottish surname name made truly special by that final "x." The worldwide fame of British boxer — World and Olympic champion — Lennox Claudius Lewis brought the name into the spotlight as a first name, while as a last it's tied to Eurythmics singer Annie L.

The Thane of Lennox appears in *Macbeth*, Mary Lennox is in *The Secret Garden* and there are two Agatha Christie characters with the name.

Lenox is another accepted spelling.

Leo

Latin, "lion"

Leo is a strong-yet-friendly name that was common among the Romans, used for thirteen popes, and is now on the upswing partly thanks to Leonardo "Leo" DiCaprio. Penelope Cruz and Javier Bardem, and actress Kim Raver called their sons Leo, as did NASCAR driver Jeff Gordon and Kristin Olson.

Leo has a lot of elements going for it: its leonine associations suggest strength of character and physique, its zodiac reference appeals to New Agers, and its "o" ending gives it added energy.

Famous Leos of the past include Pope Leo the Great and twelve other popes, a number of early saints, and Leo Tolstoy, as well as Dead End Kid Gorcey, colorful baseball manager Durocher, influential gallerist Castelli and the leonine MGM icon. There have been Leos seen on everything from *The West Wing* to *Charmed* to *Grey's Anatomy* to *Seinfeld.*

Leo is on an international roll — it is currently in the Top 20 in both France (where it's pronounced LAY-o) and Sweden.

Leon

Greek variation of Leo, "lion"

Leon is one of the leonine names that are extremely hot in Europe right now — it's been the top name in Germany and Number 2 in Switzerland. And though it peaked here in the 1920s, it is slowly making its way back, now at Number 357, and it could climb further with parents wanting a more serious and studious alternative to Leo.

Russian Marxist Revolutionary Lev Davidovich Bronstein is known to history as Leon Trotsky, Leon (LAY-on) has been the name of three French prime ministers and is currently in the news via Secretary of Defense and CIA Director Leon Panetta; Leon Russell is a respected singer-songwriter — and Brad and Angelina did use Leon for their twin son Knox's middle name.

Leonardo

Italian and Spanish variation of Leonard, "strong as a lion"

For centuries this name was associated primarily with the towering figure of Italian Renaissance painter-scientist-inventor Leonardo da Vinci, and was scarcely used outside the Latin culture. But then along came Leonardo DiCaprio, who was supposedly given the name because his pregnant mother felt her first kick while looking at a da Vinci painting in the Uffizi Gallery in Florence, and who would make the name young and handsome and multi-cultural.

Leonardo is, along with other attractive Italian and Spanish names, rising rapidly, now at Number 150, and bringing nickname Leo along with it.

Leopold

German, "brave people"

This aristocratic, somewhat formal Germanic route to the popular Leo is a royal name: Queen Victoria used it to honor a favorite uncle, King Leopold of Belgium. Though Leopold sounds as if it might be a leonine name, it's not really a relative of such choices as Leon, and Leonard.

In literature, the name is famous via Leopold Bloom, the central character of James Joyce's *Ulysses* and in music is associated with the distinguished conductor Leopold Stokowski, and is also a saint's name.

Lev

Hebrew; Russian, "heart; lion"

This concise one-syllable name, Hebrew for heart or the Russian form of Leo, has definite potential, being more unusual than the increasingly popular Levi.

The leonine Lev is the Russian birth name of the great novelist Tolstoy, and the mother of Liev Schreiber has stated that she named him in honor of the writer. In the Chaim Potok novel *My Name is Asher Lev*, about a Hasidic Jewish boy in New York, Lev is the character's surname.

Actress Candace Cameron has a son she named Lev.

Levi

Hebrew, "joined, attached"

Levi, lighter and more energetic than most biblical names, with its up vowel ending, combines Old Testament gravitas with the casual flair associated with Levi Strauss jeans.

Now being rediscovered in a major way — Levi has shot up to Number 55, its highest yet — especially after receiving a lot of attention as the sons of Matthew McConaughey, Sheryl Crow and Sara Gilbert — and as Bristol Palin's former beau, Levi Johnston.

In the Old Testament, Levi was the third son of Leah and Jacob, from whom the priestly tribe of Levites descended; in the New Testament, Levi was Matthew's given name before he became an apostle. In the Thomas Hardy novel *Far from the Madding Crowd*, Levi Everdene is the father of the heroine. Levon is a related name.

Lewis

English variation of Louis, "renowned warrior"

Lewis, the more formal and phonetic spelling of the French Louis, has been the Number 1 or 2 name in Scotland since 2000, and is one that parents in the U.S. are just beginning to rethink.

Lewis was a Top 100 name in this country from 1880 to 1930, reaching Number 30 in 1880. One of its most famous namesakes is Lewis Carroll — born Charles; a current bearer is comedian Lewis Black. Lewis is also a very common surname, as in Lewis & Clark, Jerry Lewis, Jerry Lee Lewis, Daniel Day Lewis, Sinclair Lewis, Leona Lewis, and many other notables. Louis Armstrong pronounced his first name as Lewis.

Nickname/middle name Lou is making a comeback for girls (as in Keri Russell's Willa Lou), so why not Lew for boys?

Liam

Irish short form of William, "resolute protection"

Liam began as a short form of William, but has long stood on its own. It is now one of the fastest-rising Irish names in the US, climbing 9 places in the last year to break into the Top 10 for the first time ever.

Irish-born actor Liam Neeson was instrumental in driving Liam up the charts, as was, to a lesser degree, former Oasis member Liam (born William) Gallagher. Celebrities who have chosen Liam for their sons include Tori Spelling, Calista Flockhart, Rod Stewart, Kevin Costner and Craig Ferguson.

Internationally, Liam is enjoying great popularity not only in the US and Ireland (where it's Number 15), but Scotland and Sweden (Number 9) and Australia (14).

Jaunty and richly textured, Liam is sure to increase even further in popularity.

Lincoln

English, "town by the pool"

This admirable presidential choice with a stylish two-syllable sound projects the tall, rangy, upright, image of Honest Abe. Bill Murray is father to a son named Lincoln, and Kathryn Erbe's boy Carson has Lincoln for middle name. Kristen Bell and Dax Shepard made the surprising choice of Lincoln for their daughter.

Lincoln Steffens was an influential muckraking writer, author of *The Shame of the Cities*.

The nickname Linc has a nice 60s *Mod Squad* feel.

Linus

Greek, "flax"

Can Linus lose its metaphorical security blanket and move from the Peanuts page onto the birth certificate? We think it has enough charm and other positive elements going for it for the answer to be yes, and many other parents are starting to agree.

In Greek myth, Linus is both a musician and poet, the inventor of rhythm and melody who taught music to Hercules. In the Christian era, Linus was the name of the second pope, Saint Peter's successor, while in modern times chemist Linus Pauling was awarded the Nobel Prize twice.

Humphrey Bogart as Linus Larrabee won the heart of Audrey Hepburn in *Sabrina*, and Matt Damon played Linus Caldwell in three of the *Oceans* movies.

Linus is currently in or around the Top 50 in Germany, Sweden and Norway.

Lionel

Latin, "young lion"

Lionel is one leonine name that hasn't taken off as cousins Leo and Leonardo have, though it did reenter the Top 1000 in 2010 after several years away; it was at its highest point in the 1920s and 1930s.

This French diminutive of Leon has had many worthy namesakes over time, including Sir Lionel, a Knight of the Round Table, actor Barrymore, critic Trilling, musicians Hampton and Richie, Argentine Olympic footballer Messi, and characters in numerous movies and TV shows — the real life speech therapist Lionel Logue was portrayed in *The King's Speech*.

Lionel Barrymore, of the famed theatrical family, was a mainstay of Golden Age Hollywood films, and kids might like the association to Lionel trains.

This is a timeless choice worth considering.

Llewellyn

Welsh, "resembling a lion"

Llewellyn is a common patriotic first name in Wales, with its distinctive Welsh double "LL"s; in the U.S. Llewellyn would make a daring choice, though with the chance that some might find the *ellen* sound slightly feminine.

Two princes who played a great role in the medieval Welsh quest for independence were Llewelyn Fawr (Llewelyn the Great) and Llywelyn yr Olaf (Llywelyn the Last).

Llewelyn Moss is a major character in Cormac McCarthy's *No Country for Old Men*, played on screen by Josh Brolin.

Llewellyn, which can be spelled in a number of ways, has some appealing, if quirky, short forms as well — Llew, Lleu and Llelo.

Logan

Scottish, "small hollow"

Logan is a bright and cheerful Scottish surname that originated from a place of that name in Ayrshire. Logan has been climbing steadily since the mid-70s; it was in the Top 20 from 2006 to 2011, but is at Number 21 now and could be slowing its rise. Not surprisingly, Logan is mega-popular in its native Scotland — now Number 5 — but also in Canada, ranking Number 5 in 2012.

The mutant character Wolverine, known as Logan, based on the X-Men comics and played by Hugh Jackman on film, has had a considerable impact on the name. There were also attractive guys named Logan on *Veronica Mars* and *Gilmore Girls*.

Logan is also used for girls, but less so now than it was in the mid-90s.

Lorcan

Irish, "little, fierce"
Lorcan is a name rich in Irish history as belonging to several kings, including the grandfather of the most famous high king of Ireland, Brian Boru. Lorcan O'Toole, known in English as Laurence O'Toole, is the patron saint of Dublin, so it's not too surprising that Irish-born actor Peter O'Toole named his son Lorcan.

In the *Harry Potter* epic, Lorcan is the twin son of Luna Lovegood Scamander.

Strong, easy to pronounce and spell, Lorcan is an Irish name that would stand out from the more common crop of Connors and Liams.

Lorenzo

Italian variation of Laurence, "from Laurentium"
Latinizing Lawrence gives it a whole new lease on life. Like Leonardo, Lorenzo has been integrated into the American stockpot of names, partly via actor Lorenzo Lamas. Other associations are with Lorenzo de' Medici, the Florentine Renaissance merchant prince and art patron, Renaissance artists Ghiberti and Lotto, and the upstanding young man who married Shylock's daughter Jessica in Shakespeare's *The Merchant of Venice*.

Lorenzo has been steadily in the 2 – 300 range on the popularity lists in the US, is currently Number 4 in its native Italy, and is also hot in France. It would work well with a simple one-syllable Anglo name — in the depths of radio history, there was a soap opera character named Lorenzo Jones.

Renzo is an appealing nickname, sometimes used on its own.

Louis

German and French, "renowned warrior"
While this classic royal name has yet to catch on in the U.S., we sense a comeback. Both Louis and Lewis are in Britain's Top 100, and if they don't revive here, all the better for those — like actors Sandra Bullock and Bill Pullman — with the good taste to choose Louis for their sons.

Louis was the name of sixteen kings of France, and with this French spelling may be pronounced as Louie. Using the English spelling Lewis may solve that issue, though we think the Louis version is more elegant.

Lowell

French, "young wolf"

Lowell is an upstanding and somewhat conservative name that calls to mind the genteel patrician families of nineteenth-century New England, such as the one poet Robert Lowell was born into. Two other Lowell-surnamed poets are Amy and James Russell.

Lowell was at its height in the 1930s, when it reached Number 148, and has been off the list since 1986 — long enough to deserve a reappraisal.

Namesakes include Governor Lowell P. Weicker of Connecticut and noted newsman Lowell Thomas; on TV Lowells have been featured on *Wings* and *Sons of Anarchy*.

An interesting British upper-class spelling is Loel.

Loyal

English, "faithful, loyal"

Loyal is one of the few virtue names suitable for boys, an honorable and principled Boy Scout-esque appellation with a surprisingly long and distinguished history.

Loyal was a mid-list name at the end of the nineteenth century, reaching Number 555 in 1890. It has been on hiatus since 1948 — and this might be the moment to bring it back as an unusual but usable choice with real meaning. Loyal probably originally signified devotion to country rather than person, but in either case, fidelity is a great attribute to impart to a child. And who knows? Maybe Loy could be the new Roy.

Luc

French variation of Luke, "man from Lucania"

Luc is the sexier Gallic cousin of Luke, and if you want to know the difference between their pronunciations, just watch Kevin Kline's hilarious description in the film *French Kiss*. Peter Gabriel and Sean Patrick Thomas picked this version for their sons — which would also make a cool middle name.

Luca

Italian variation of Luke, "man from Lucania"

If there was once a bias against this charming and venerable Italian name for possibly sounding too feminine, consider it gone. Since Luca entered the boys' US popularity list in 2000, it has scooted up more than 300 places to Number 223. Popular throughout Europe as well, Luca is currently Number 12 in its native Italy, and in the Top 25 in Austria, Belgium and The Netherlands.

Colin Firth and his Italian wife chose Luca for one of their sons, as did Vincent d'Onofrio.

Lucas

Latin form of Luke, "man from Lucania"
Lucas is steadily inching up in popularity with parents who want something similar to but more substantial than Luke, to the point where it ranks Number 27, its highest place ever.

Lucas has long been a favorite of TV scriptwriters, from the early black-and-white days of *The Rifleman* (Chuck Connors as Lucas McCain) to the schoolteacher series *Lucas Tanner* to the more recent *One Tree Hill*, and the name appears as Lucas Beauchamp in William Faulkner's *Intruder in the Dust* and *Light in August*.

Lucas Cranach was an important German Renaissance painter and printmaker; Lucas Samaras is an eccentric Greek-born American contemporary artist. Some will associate the name with director George Lucas.

At the moment Lucas is enjoying a tremendous international success. It is currently the Number 2 name in France and Belgium, Number 3 in Sweden and Canada, and Number 4 in the Netherlands.

Lucian

Latin, "light"
Lucian is a sleeker, more sophisticated version of Lucius that is climbing in tandem with other "Lu"-starting names.

Historically, the name was made famous by the ancient Greek satirist Lucian of Samosata — sometimes considered the father of science fiction — and by the third-century St. Lucian.

A modern bearer was Berlin-born British painter Lucian Freud, grandson of Sigmund. In pop culture, Lucian the Lycan is a werewolf in the Underworld movies.

Lucian was picked for his son by Indie actor Steve Buscemi. Lucien is the French version.

Lucius

Latin, "light"
Lucius is an exotic old Roman clan name that has lots of religious and literary resonance, yet is still vital today. It was the name of three popes, appears in several Shakespeare plays, and, like all the names beginning with "luc" relates to the Latin word for light. It was one of a limited number of forenames used in ancient Rome.

In the Bible, Lucius is the name of three people; Shakespeare used it for the son of Titus in *Titus Andronicus*, a young servant of Brutus in *Julius Caesar*, a lord in *Timon of Athens* and a Roman general in *Cymbeline*.

Other fictional bearers of the name can be found in *Le Morte d'Arthur*, *The Golden Ass*, Ralph Ellison's *Invisible Man*, Faulkner's *The Reivers*, *Batman*, *Talladega Nights*, and *The Incredibles*. Lucius Malfoy, the father of Draco, is a Harry Potter villain, and other Luciuses have been portrayed on screen by Morgan Freeman, Joaquin Phoenix, and Luke Wilson.

Real life namesakes include renowned World War II General Lucius B. Clay, and writer, photographer and bon vivant Lucius Beebe.

Luke

Greek, "man from Lucania"

Luke is a cool-yet-strong New Testament name, with a relaxed cowboy feel, which has been on the rise since the advent of Luke Skywalker.

The most famous bearer of the name is the first-century Greek physician, evangelist, and friend of Saint Paul, the author of the third Gospel, who was also supposed to have been a portrait painter. He thus became the patron saint of doctors and artists. Later Lukes of less note have been Luke Duke of *The Dukes of Hazzard*, *Cool Hand Luke*, half of the classic soap-opera duo of Luke and Laura, contemporary actors Luke Wilson and Luke Perry, and a number of star athletes.

Luke is currently in the U.S. Top 40, and is even more popular in Ireland, where it's Number 12.

Lysander

Greek, "liberator"

Lysander is a distinctive Greek name that could be thought of as a more creative cousin of Alexander. In ancient history, Lysander was the name of an esteemed Spartan naval commander and his literary cred comes from one of the two star-struck young men in Shakespeare's *A Midsummer Night's Dream*, as well as one of the twin sons (the other being Lorcan) of Luna Lovegood, whom we learn about in the *Harry Potter* epilogue.

Previously confined to the nurseries of Mayfair and Belgravia, we think Lysander could easily emigrate to the playgrounds of Park Slope.

M

Mack

Scottish, diminutive of names beginning with "Mac" or "Mc," meaning "son of""

Mack, when "formalized" with the final "k," makes an engagingly amiable choice, a far more uncommon option to the ubiquitous Max, with a nice, every-guy feel. Mack entered the popularity lists briefly in 2009 for the first time since 1989; it was a Top 100 name in 1900.

Mack (born Michael) Sennett was the innovator of slapstick comedy in silent films. The name is also suggestive of Mack the Knife and a whole family of computers. Kevin Kline, Cuba Gooding, Jr, Dan Aykroyd, Eric Roberts and Snoop Dogg have all played characters named Mack.

But we also like Mac, which can be a friendly short form for names from Macallister to Macon to Macarius.

Macon

French place-name

What with Mason scooting up the charts, this attractive place-name, with its thick Georgia accent, could make a more distinctive alternative.

Macon has played major roles in two novels, Anne Tyler's *The Accidental Tourist* and Toni Morrison's *Song of Solomon*, in the latter as both a Macon Sr and Jr

Maddox

Welsh, "son of Madoc"

Maddox, a previously obscure Welsh family name with a powerfully masculine image, suddenly came into the spotlight when Angelina Jolie chose it for her son in 2003. By the following year it was in the middle of the Top 1000, and by 2012 had reached Number 166, with more than two thousand baby boys inheriting the name.

It was Maddox who set the precedent for all the boys in the Jolie-Pitt clan to have names ending in "x"-and helped fuel the spark for all names "X."

Maddox is related to the traditional Welsh Madoc (pronounced MAH-dog), meaning "fortunate"; it belonged to a bearer who, according to legend, colonized North America in the twelfth century.

Maddox is a character in *The Vampire Diaries*; spelled Madox, it appeared in Michael Ondaatje's *The English Patient*.

Magnus

Latin, "greatest"

Magnus, a powerful name with a commanding presence, is one of the newly unearthed ancient artifacts; it dates back to Charlemagne being called Carolus Magnus, or Charles the Great. It was picked for their sons by Will Ferrell (whose wife Viveca Paulin is Swedish), Kirsty Swanson and Elizabeth Banks.

A royal appellation in Scandinavia, Magnus was the name of six early kings of Norway and four of Sweden; it is still a Top 6 name in Denmark and Norway.

Magnus has made appearances as a vampire in Anne Rice's *Vampire Chronicles* and as a character in Roald Dahl's *Matilda*. And for an extra ego boost, in Charles Dickens's *The Pickwick Papers*, there's the following dialogue: "Magnus is my name. It's rather a good name, I think, sir." "A very good name, indeed," said Mr. Pickwick.

Malachi

Hebrew, "my messenger"

An Old Testament name with a Gaelic lilt that's definitely on the rise; Malachi entered the list in 1987, and has been in the Top 200 since 2003.

In the Bible, Malachi (pronounced with the final syllable as EYE), was the last of the twelve Hebrew prophets, who foretold the coming of Christ.

In Anthony Trollope's *Phineas Finn*, Malachi is the name of the hero's father, and in James Joyce's *Ulysses*, Malachi Mulligan is a medical student.

Malachy

Irish version of Malachi, Hebrew, "my messenger"

This spelling, which came to the attention of readers of the best-selling *Angela's Ashes* as the name of author Frank McCourt's father and brother, the latter of whom wrote a best-seller of his own, lends the biblical name a more expansive, almost boisterous image. Malachy is also the anglicized version of Melaghlin, one of St. Patrick's first companions. It was borne by the High King Malachy, who defeated the Vikings at the Battle of Tara in 980. St. Malachy was a reformer who reorganized the church in Ireland after the Viking raids. Irish actor Cillian Murphy has a son named Malachy.

Malcolm

Scottish, "devotee of St. Colomba"

Malcolm is a warm and welcoming Scottish appellation (originally Mael-Colium) that fits into that golden circle of names that are distinctive but not at all odd. A royal name in Scotland, Malcolm is also a hero name for many via radical civil rights activist Malcolm X.

Malcolm was the name of four Scottish kings — including the son of Duncan who succeeded to the throne after Macbeth murdered his father — and has been a standard in that country.

Denzel Washington named one of his sons Malcolm, as did Harrison Ford.

Actor Malcolm McDowell is one current bearer; other possible namesakes are writer Lowry, bestselling author and trendspotter Gladwell, media mogul Forbes, Sex Pistols musician McLaren and actor Jamal Warner. There have also been several Malcolms on TV — e.g., in *Malcolm in the Middle*, *Firefly* — and in the *Outlander* series. There were no less than three characters named Malcolm in the *Harry Potter* books.

Malo

Breton, "shining hostage"

Malo, the name of an important sixth-century Breton saint who founded St. Malo, the charming port town in Brittany — is considered quite au courant in France right now, ranking firmly in the Top 100.

Saint Malo of Aleth, a patron saint of lost items, was consecrated the first Bishop of Aleth. He was also known as Maclou, Maclovius and, in Italian, Macuto. Malo is worth thinking about as a highly unusual alternative to Milo.

Marco

Italian and Spanish form of Mark, "warlike"

Simple and universal, Marco is a Latin classic that would make a much livelier namesake for an Uncle Mark. It was used for her son by actress Jill Hennessy, and goes well with any straightforward surname.

Marco, related to the Roman god Mars, has long been associated with Marco Polo, the thirteenth-century Venetian merchant-traveler who was instrumental in introducing Europeans to Asian culture. Eugene O'Neill wrote a play called *Marco Millions*, based on the life of Marco Polo.

More recent noteworthy Marcos are Marco Andretti, Indy race car driver grandson of the legendary Mario, and Marco Rubio, Florida senator, and the name can also be found in two early Dr. Seuss books.

Marco retains its long-term popularity in Italy.

Marcus

Latin, "warlike"

Well over two thousand parents chose this ancient Roman name for their sons in the last year recorded, some perhaps honoring Marcus Garvey, leader of the Back to Africa movement. Though ancient, Marcus now sounds more current than Mark, in tune with today's trend towards "us" ending Latinate names.

Marcus was commonplace in classical Rome — not surprising as it was one of only about a dozen given names in use then. Among the most prominent were the emperor and stoic philosopher Marcus Aurelius, the Marcus known to us as Mark Antony, and the politician, philosopher and orator Cicero.

Dr. Marcus Welby was a staple on vintage TV, and since then we have seen the name on both the *Harry Potter* and *Twilight* franchises, as the protagonist of Nick Hornby's *About a Boy*, on *Sons of Anarchy* and *Men of a Certain Age*, and in *Indiana Jones*, *The Blind Side*, and *Bad Santa*.

Marcus Loew was the movie magnate behind MGM and Loew's theatres, and Marcus Allen was an Oakland Raiders superstar.

Marius is a related possibility.

Marino

Latin, "of the sea"

Marino is an Italian first and surname with distinct crossover possibilities, having pleasant seaside undertones, and is far more unusual in the U.S. than sister Marina.

Marino Marini was an Italian sculptor who has a museum dedicated to his work in Florence; Dan Marino a record-breaking football quarterback.

Marlon

English, meaning unknown

Associated for half a century with Marlon Brando, who inherited the French-inflected name from his father, Marlon has been especially well used by African-Americans, including the Jackson and Wayans families. Though heard much less now than it was in the 70s, this could change as parents look to the names of old Hollywood stars.

Keith Richards, Dennis Miller, and (more recently) Money Mazur all have sons named Marlon.

Martin

Latin, "warlike"

Martin is one of those names like Arthur and Vincent and George that is in the process of throwing off its balding middle-aged image to start sounding possible again, used in full without the dated Marty nickname.

Notable Martins are too numerous to mention as the name has been so well used throughout time and in so many countries. Martin became part of the basic European stock of names largely due to the popularity of the fourth-century St. Martin of Tours. Also influential were the German founder of Protestantism Martin Luther and civil rights leader Martin Luther King (originally born Michael and renamed in honor of Martin Luther), eighth President Martin Van Buren, and influential philosophers Heidegger and Buber.

More current Martins include actors Sheen and Short, writer Amis, and director Scorsese; *Martin Chuzzlewit* by Dickens and *Martin Eden* by Jack London are part of its literary legacy.

Martin is enjoying popularity in several far-flung countries — it's Number 4 in Chile, and in the Top 50 in Spain, France, Hungary, and Norway.

Yes, a Martin revival appears to be right around the corner — if only we can think of a new nickname.

Mason

English occupational name, "worker in stone"
Mason has become mega-popular, hitting the Number 2 spot in 2011, by far the highest it's ever been on the Social Security list.

Mason is an occupational surname that's been heating up for several years, a fresher sounding replacement for the Jason we've moved way beyond, in step with the newer style Cason/Kason.

Mason has been getting a lot of reality-show media attention since it was chosen by Kourtney Kardashian for her son, but it's been used by several other celebs as well, including Cuba Gooding, Jr, Melissa Joan Hart and Kevin Richardson (as well as by Kelsey Grammer for his daughter).

Recently there have been two cute TV werewolves named Mason: Mason Greyback on *Wizards of Waverly Place* and Mason Lockwood on *Vampire Diaries* — a far cry from the name's wholesome image.

Matteo

Italian variation of Matthew, "gift of God"
This attractively energetic Italian version of the classic Matthew is primed to move further and further into mainstream American nomenclature; in terms of popularity, it

has risen to Number 412, while the Spanish spelling, Mateo, is at Number 138. Not surprisingly, both rank high in their native countries: Matteo is Number 5 in Italy, Mateo 34 in Spain.

Actor Colin Firth has a son called Matteo, as does Ricky Martin; the Benjamin Bratts and Tom Colicchios have boys named Mateo. We're sure that both these spellings will keep climbing in tandem, sharing the possibility of the lively nickname Teo.

Matthias

Aramaic variation of Matthew, "gift of God"
With Matthew sounding somewhat exhausted, and ancient endings sounding new again, this New Testament apostolic name makes an appealing and recommended choice. Both Mathias and Matias are well used in the Hispanic community, and throughout Europe. Will Ferrell and his Swedish wife chose Matias for their second son.

In the Bible, Matthias is the apostle chosen to replace Judas Iscariot. The Catholic and Eastern Orthodox churches honor Matthias as a saint.

The Mathias spelling is used by George Eliot for the father of the protagonist of her novel *Adam Bede*.

Matthias is currently a Top 25 name in Austria, and is also well used in France, The Netherlands and Belgium.

Max

English and German diminutive of Maximilian or Maxwell, "greatest"
Max was transformed from cigar-chomping grandpa to rosy-cheeked baby in the 1980s, along with card-playing partners Sam and Jake.

Never quite as popular as it seemed, Max is now, at Number 105, close to the highest it's been on the Social Security list since 1917, when German-sounding names went out of favor. The character named Max in the children's classic *Where the Wild Things Are* had an impact on baby namers. Max is currently in the Top 20 in Britain, Australia, Germany, The Netherlands, Australia and New Zealand.

Max has been a popular starbaby name for decades, most recently for the sons of Christina Aguilera, Cynthia Nixon and Charlie Sheen, while other celebs, such as Jennifer Lopez and Marc Anthony, have used more formal appellations — Maximilian, Maxwell, Maxfield — on the birth certificate to get to the nickname Max. Skater Scott Hamilton put his own spin on it by maximizing the spelling of his son's name to Maxx.

Warning: Max has long been the top name for canines.

Maximus

Latin, "greatest"

The powerful name of the powerful character played by Russell Crowe in the 2000 film *Gladiator* first appeared on the popularity charts that same year. It's Max to the max. One time considered a "too much name" name, Maximus has entered the realm of possibility — enough so that there were close to two thousand boys given that name last year.

Maximus was originally a Latin title of honor given to successful military commanders, such as Quintus Fabius Maximus, and then came to be a personal name, borne by several early saints.

In George Eliot's novel *Felix Holt: The Radical*, Maximus Debarry is very much an aristocrat.

Mercer

French occupational name, "a merchant"

Mercer is an attractive possibility which is an occupational name that doesn't sound like one. Mercer and its cool, sophisticated short form Merce project a super creative image via their artistic namesakes.

Johnny Mercer was a talented and charming songwriter-singer who wrote the lyrics for more than 1,500 songs, including *Moon River*. Jazz great Duke Ellington named his son Mercer, and he in turn became a respected musician in his own right. Stone Temple Pilot's Scott Weiland used Mercer as the middle name of his son Noah.

In the visual arts, Mercer Mayer is a prolific children's book writer and illustrator.

The short form Merce is associated with avant garde dancer/choreographer Merce Cunningham, born Mercier, whose name still resonates with an aura of bold originality.

Micah

Hebrew, "who is like the Lord"

Micah is a biblical name which growing numbers of parents are looking at as a more unusual alternative to Michael, projecting a shinier, more lively image.

Micah is the name of a biblical prophet and was used fairly frequently by the seventeenth-century pilgrims. It is also the name of the central character in Arthur Conan Doyle's historical, non-Holmes novel, *Micah Clarke*, and Micah Sanders was a child prodigy character on *Heroes*.

Everwood/Grey's Anatomy actress Sarah Drew named her son Micah.

And although Micah will probably never reach Michael's Number 1 spot, be aware that it's now just outside the Top 100, and advancing every year.

Miles

Latin, "a soldier" or German, "merciful, generous"

Miles, which took on a permanent veneer of cool thanks to jazz great Miles Davis, is a confident and polished name that has been appreciated in particular by celebrity baby namers, including Elisabeth Shue, Mayim Bialik, Larenz Tate, Joan Cusack and Lionel Ritchie. Ranking at Number 111, it is by far at its highest point ever.

Miles was the name of the first translator of the Bible into English — the English monk Miles Coverdale, which is also the name of a character in Hawthorne's *The Blithedale Romance*. Miles Hendon figures in Mark Twain's *The Prince and the Pauper*, and Miles was one of the young children in Henry James's *The Turn of the Screw*. Miles — or Myles — Standish was the leader of the Pilgrim fathers.

Miles has also been a favorite movie and TV character name from the days of *Murphy Brown* to *24* and *Avatar*.

Miller

English occupational name, "grinder of grain"

Miller is an up-and-coming choice in the stylish occupational genre, chosen by Stella McCartney, Melissa Etheridge, and by Téa Leoni and David Duchovny.

Though relatively rare as a first name, Miller is the seventh most common surname in America, so there are innumerable Miller namesakes, including writers Arthur and Henry, and entertainers Dennis, Glenn, Jonny Lee, Larry, Mitch, Roger, Steve and Sienna. And in fiction, there's Henry James's heroine, Daisy Miller.

Milo

Latinized and Old German form of Miles," a soldier; or merciful, generous"

Milo has long been a highly recommended author favorite, now getting some well-deserved appreciation. With its German, Greek and jaunty Anglo/Irish input, Milo combines the strength of the ancient Greek Olympic wrestler of that name — a six-time winner of the Olympic games — with the debonair charm of a WW II RAF pilot.

More recently, Milo has been associated with the dashing Milo Ventimiglia, of *Heroes* fame, and has also been a character in *Catch-22* and *The Phantom Tollbooth*, on screen in *Milo and Otis*, *Alias*, and *Atlantis: The Lost Empire*.

Ricki Lake, Camryn Manheim, Sherry Stringfield, Liv Tyler and Alyssa Milano are five celebrity moms who share our enthusiasm for Milo, as do many Nameberry baby namers.

Milo is often heard in Ireland.

Moe

English, diminutive of Moses, "delivered from the water"

If Gus and Max have made it, why not Moe? Can it be the lingering Three Stooges effect? We think that Moe, like Joe, is one of the friendliest and most open of regular guy nickname names and should get a little more appreciation.

There have been some very visible on-screen Moes, such as Moe Green in *The Godfather* and Moe Szyskak on *The Simpsons*, proprietor of Moe's Tavern.

The real life Moe (born Morris) Berg was a fascinating character, a Major League baseball player called "the brainiest guy in baseball" who later served as a spy during World War II.

Morris

English variation of Maurice, "dark-skinned"

Morris is as quiet and comfortable as a Morris chair, and has the same vintage feel. Once a Top 100 name in the early 1900s, Morris fell completely off the roster in 1995, probably due to lingering fallout from his identification with Morris the cat's ("the world's most finicky cat") 9 Lives cat food commercials.

A more distinguished namesake is Morris (Mo) Udall, an influential congressman, and, from literature, Morris Townsend in the Henry James novel *Washington Square*, which was made into a movie titled *The Heiress*, with Montgomery Clift playing the part.

The usual nicknames for Morris are Morrie/Maury or Moe; a more distinctive one would be Moss. Morrie Schwartz, subject of the bestseller *Tuesdays with Morrie*, was born Morris.

Morrissey

Irish, "descendant of Muiris"

When British rocker Steven Patrick Morrissey decided to use his last name alone, it became a viable option for baby namers, a lot cooler than Morris or Maurice, with the nice three-syllable lilt of such other Irish surnames as Finnegan and Flanagan. It can also be spelled Morrisey.

Morrison is a related possibility, also with musical ties, to Irish singer-songwriter Van (born George Ivan).

Moses

Egyptian, "delivered from the water"

Gwyneth Paltrow and Chris Martin's choice of this white-bearded Old Testament name helped bring it into the modern age, along with brethren Elijah, Isaiah, and Isaac. User-friendly nicknames include Moe and Mose.

The biblical story of Moses is, of course, one of the most familiar from the Old Testament — Moses being found as a baby in the bulrushes, growing up to lead the Israelites out of Egyptian bondage and into the Promised Land, then bringing down the Ten Commandments from Mount Sinai.

Moshe, as in Israeli statesman Dayan, is the Yiddish form of the name. In Spanish, it is Moises.

A namesake from the world of sports is NBA Hall of Famer Moses Malone; Mose Allison is a jazz blues pianist and singer.

Moss

English, "descendant of Moses"; word name

This evocative green nature name, heard much more frequently as a surname, is associated with playwright Moss Hart (born Robert), who co-wrote (with George S. Kaufman) such enduring Broadway comedies as *The Man Who Came to Dinner* and *You Can't Take it With You.*

Never having made it onto the popularity list, Moss would make a distinctively fresh and attractive alternative to Ross.

Prominent bearers of Moss as a surname include British auto racer Stirling, supermodel Kate, and Elisabeth Moss, best known as Peggy Olson on *Mad Men.*

Murphy

Irish, "sea warrior"

This jaunty Celtic surname — the most common family name in Ireland — is totally viable as a first. Although there was a possibility of its being feminized via the old TV sitcom *Murphy Brown,* it has never taken off for girls and very much retains its masculine image.

There have been countless notable surnamed Murphys, including the currently prominent Eddie and Cillian. Murphy was the eponymous protagonist of Samuel Beckett's first published novel.

One possible negative: the association with Murphy's Law — if anything can go wrong, it will.

N

Nash

English, "by the ash tree"

Nash is an English surname whose sound puts it right in step with currently trendy names like Cash, Dash, and Ash. It first came to prominence via TV character Nash Bridges, portrayed by Don Johnson in the late 90s, and also by mathematician John Nash, played by Russell Crowe in the acclaimed film *A Beautiful Mind*. Nash first entered the popularity list in 1997, and is now at Number 521.

As a surname, Nash has been associated with witty poet Ogden (born Frederic Ogden), auto manufacturer Charles, maker of the defunct brand, and rock musician Graham, of Crosby, Stills and Nash — as well as Clarence "Ducky" Nash, the voice of Donald Duck. Iron Chef Cat Cora named her son Nash Lemuel.

Nathan

Hebrew, "given"

Nathan is an Old Testament name that's been steadily on the upswing for forty years and is now at Number 29. Strong, solid, and attractive, Nathan was chosen for his son by Jon Stewart. It's a name familiar to every schoolchild through Nathan Hale, the Revolutionary War spy.

In the Old Testament, Nathan was the name of a prophet and also that of one of King David's sons. It is mega popular in Europe right now, the Number 1 name in France and Number 3 in Belgium.

Nat and Nate (as featured on TV shows like *Six Feet Under* and *Gossip Girl*) are just the kind of friendly, old-fashioned nicknames that are now very much in style.

Nathans have starred in some classic films — it was the name of the character played by Kevin Kline in *Sophie's Choice*, by Jack Nicholson in *A Few Good Men*, and Frank Sinatra was Nathan Detroit in the film version of *Guys and Dolls*. Nathan Zuckerman is the protagonist of several novels by Philip Roth.

In the public eye right now is Nathan Fillion, who portrays TV's Castle.

Nathaniel

Hebrew, "gift of God"

Although Nathan is more popular, the more dignified Nathaniel is firmly in the Top 100 and has been since the 1980s. Despite the profusion of Nat names around, Nathaniel remains singularly appealing and distinctive, with several attractive nicknames — Nat, Natty and Nate. Parents finding it overused might opt for New Testament Apostle Nathaniel's other name, Bartholomew.

A boy named Nathaniel would have any number of real life and literary namesakes to inspire him. These include Revolutionary General Nathanael Greene, rebel slave Nat Turner, writers Nathaniel Hawthorne and Nathanael (born Nathan) West, lithographer Nathaniel Currier, partner of Ives, and singer/pianist Nat "King" Cole.

An early literary character with the name is Sir Nathaniel in Shakespeare's *Love's Labour's Lost*, and then there was Natty Bumpo in James Fenimore Cooper's *Leatherstocking Tales* and Nathaniel Winkle in Dickens's *The Pickwick Papers*.

In the realm of pop culture, we find such Nathaniels as Nate Fisher in *Six Feet Under*, and others in *The Wire*, *Gossip Girl*, and *Enchanted*, as well as the protagonist of the *Pirates of the Caribbean* video, Nathaniel Hawk.

Ned

English, diminutive of Edward, "wealthy guardian"

Ned is a gently old-fashioned Nancy Drew-Bobbsey Twins-era short form for Edward that sounds cooler than Ed and is enjoying a small style renaissance.

Usage of Ned in literature goes back to a Ben Johnson character in 1614, and it is also the name of the protagonist in James Fenimore Cooper's *Ned Myers*. In Australia, Ned Kelly is famous as a larger-than-life legendary outlaw figure. In this country, Ned Rorem is a respected modern composer.

There was a 1990s sitcom called *Ned and Stacey*, and other Neds have appeared in *The Simpsons* (neighbor Flanders), *Groundhog Day* and *School of Rock*.

Nehemiah

Hebrew, "comforted by God"

Nehemiah is an Old Testament name, used by the Puritans, whose white-bearded image kept it out of favor for centuries, until it suddenly reappeared in 1998, along with the more user-friendly Josiah and Isaiah; it is now Number 342.

The biblical Nehemiah was the prophet assigned the rebuilding of Jerusalem after the Babylonian captivity — which could make it a fitting possibility for an architect or building contractor's boy.

In Sir Walter Scott's novel *Woodstock*, Nehemiah Holdenough is a Presbyterian minister. One modern namesake is football star Nehemiah Broughton.

Nelson

English, "son of Neil"

Nelson is a rather stiff and dated surname name that is sometimes used to honor distinguished South African activist Nelson Mandela, as Celine Dion did for one of her twin boys. Other notable associations are with British Admiral Lord Horatio Nelson, New York Governor Nelson Rockefeller, novelist Nelson Algren and movie operetta star Nelson Eddy. Nelson was also the given name of "Rabbit" Angstrom, protagonist of John Updike's series of novels.

Nelson's highest popularity was in the 1930s and 40s, when it was in the Top 200.

Niall

Irish, "champion" or "cloud"

Niall is pronounced like Neal, but this Irish spelling of the name makes it much more current and cool, and boy band One Direction's darling Niall Horan gives the name fresh celebrity gloss.

This is an ancient name borne by several of the high kings of Tara, the most famous of whom was the powerful semi-mythological fifth-century king known as Niall of the Nine Hostages, ancestor of all the O'Neills and MacNeills that followed.

Niall Ferguson is a respected English historian, one of *Time* magazine's 100 Most Influential People in the World in 2004.

Nicholas

Greek, "people of victory"

Nicholas, though it has lost some ground (it was in the Top 10 from 1993 to 2002), is still a popular classic that would make an attractive, solid choice. A Greek name stemming from Nike, the goddess of victory, it is a New Testament name also well used in literature, as in Dickens's *Nicholas Nickleby*.

And then there's St. Nicholas who, in addition to bringing bags of toys once a year, is also the patron saint of schoolchildren, mechanics, sailors, scholars, brides, bakers, travelers, and Russia, where the name was a star of the czarist dynasty.

Along with all this historical depth, Nicholas, and nicknames Nick and Nicky, project an aura of masculine panache, and has long been a favorite of writers for rich boy, Romeos, thugs and detective characters.

Offshoots Cole and Colin have long had lives of their own.

Nicholson

English, "son of Nicol"

If you're looking for a Nicholas substitute or namesake, Nicholson would make a more distinctive path to the likable nickname Nick, fitting in with other newer patronymics like Anderson and Harrison. Unusual but not outlandish, it is associated with writer Nicholson Baker, library advocate and author of *Vox*. And as a surname, of course, with Jack.

Nico

Italian diminutive of Nicholas, "people of victory"

Nico is one of the great nickname names, full of charm, energy and sex appeal — a neo Nick. It's been among highest risers on the boys' list.

Nico is commonly heard in Italy — as a short form of Niccolo — and also in France, Belgium, Germany, Holland, and Spanish-speaking countries.

As a unisex nickname name, Nico is associated with the German-born single-named Velvet Underground singer (nee Christa) promoted by Andy Warhol, and Nico Reilly was one of the female leads on the defunct TV series *Lipstick Jungle*. But over 90% of the American babies named Nico are boys.

Nicolo

Italian form of Nicholas, "people of victory"

Nicolo is a more lively and exotic variation of Nicholas. A name with a long, distinguished Italian history of its own, it also boasts the charming nickname Nico.

Although the female counterpart, Nicola, has long been a favorite in the U.K., Nicolo has not yet made a similar transition. It was chosen, though, by actor Stanley Tucci, for his son.

Nicolo is a name with musical reverberations, connected to the major early violin maker Amati, and the later violin virtuoso Paganini.

Nile

Place-name or variation of Niall, Irish, "champion"

Water names are a cool category these days, and this one of the famous Egyptian river that streamlines the fussier Niles is no exception. Nile is also related to Niall, the Irish Gaelic form of Neal/Neil.

Nile was actually used enough to make it onto the Top 1000 a couple of times around the turn of the last century.

Noah

Hebrew, "rest; wandering"

Noah, the name of the Old Testament patriarch of the ark, is one of today's unexpected fashion hits. Noah has definitely shaken off its ancient image and is now rising rapidly up the popularity charts. In 2009, Noah made it into the Top 10 for the first time in history, and now has risen to Number 5.

As every Sunday school alumnus knows, Noah was deemed the only righteous man of his time, singled out by God to survive the great flood sent to punish the wicked world: a righteous namesake. Noah has risen on the style charts along with other formerly long-beard names such as Abraham, Moses, and even Elijah, unthinkable a generation ago.

Billy Ray Cyrus, responsible for the name Miley, crossed gender lines to call another of his daughters Noah. The feminine homonym Noa — which sounds just like but is NOT a form of the biblical male Noah: but is a separate female name from the Old Testament — is currently the most popular girls' name in Israel. And Noah itself, with its vowel ending, is evidence of the trend toward softer sounds in boys' names, along with brothers Joshua and Asher.

Noam

Hebrew, "pleasantness, charm, tenderness"

Noam is an underused modern Hebrew name with any number of attractive attributes attached to its meaning; it doesn't have the biblical weight of Noah, but could make a more distinctive alternative to that popular choice. Noam is also a place-name in south Israel, where it is sometime used for girls. Its most prominent bearer is the distinguished linguist and social activist Noam Chomsky (born Avram Noam).

Noaz is an even more unusual Hebrew choice.

Noble

Latin, "aristocratic"

With parents beginning to show an interest in virtue names for boys, this Puritan favorite just might be revived, for what could be more admirable than nobility in terms of having strength of character, dignity, and high moral ideals?

Noble was actually on the Social Security list from at least 1880 to 1954, reaching as high as 312 in 1901.

Noble Sissle was an early jazz legend, noted for his collaboration with ragtime songwriter Eubie Blake.

Nolan

Irish, "champion"

Nolan is one of the rising Irish surname names, in the spirit of Conan and Ronan, partially inspired by pitcher Nolan Ryan — who was named Lynn at birth, after his father. Nolan is a cheerful, friendly traditional Irish surname with the winning meaning of "champion."

Nolan is currently just inside the Top 100, at Number 88, is well used in Canada and Belgium, and is now Number 26 in France.

Namesakes include fashion designer Nolan Miller and young Nolan Gould, who plays Luke on *Modern Family*. Comic actress Molly Shannon named her son Nolan.

North

Word name

A lot of attention was drawn to this name when Kim Kardashian and Kanye West announced it as the name of their baby daughter, making it instantly unisex. But North is a word name that's long been used, albeit very quietly, a name with a certain purity and strength. It's a good choice if you're from, say, Wisconsin or Maine, love winter or are an avid skier, or if you just want a name that's both very familiar and very unusual.

North is just one of several cool names with a directional slant — others are West, Weston, and Easton.

A young Elijah Wood played the title character in the 1994 film *North*.

O

Oak

Tree name

Oak, a symbol of solidity, strength, and longevity, is joining Cedar and Pine as a viable name, one that would work especially well in the middle.

If you'd prefer to take the longer route to the name, you can consider the surnames Oakes or Oakley.

Obadiah

Hebrew, "servant of God"

For the seriously audacious biblical baby namer who wants to move beyond Elijah and Josiah, this name has considerable old-fangled charm. Obadiah, who gave his name to one of the shortest books in the Bible, was a rich man who had the gift of prophecy. There are several other men named Obadiah in the Bible, as well as a Saint Obadiah.

In literature, there is an Obadiah in Laurence Sterne's novel *Tristan Shandy*, and another in Anthony Trollope's *Barchester Towers*.

Ocean

Nature name

Rarely heard since the hippy-dippy 60s and 70s, names like Ocean and River are flowing back into favor, especially with nature lovers and green-oriented parents.

Forest Whitaker, an inspired child namer (his other kids are called Sonnet and True), has a son named Ocean Alexander.

Variations include Oceanus, the name of the child who was born during the voyage of the Mayflower, and Oceane, a wildly popular girls' name in France.

Octavius

Latin, "eighth"

Octavius, which was at one time used for the eighth child in a family, has the worn leather patina of all the ancient Roman names now up for reconsideration.

The first Roman emperor, Augustus, was called Caius Octavius or Octavian before he took his title. He was the son of Octavius and Atia, the niece of Julius Caesar, who adopted him as his son. He appears under the name Octavius Caesar in Shakespeare's *Julius Caesar* and *Antony and Cleopatra*.

In later lit, Octavius Guy is a character in Wilkie Collins's novel *The Moonstone* and Octavius Robinson is in George Bernard Shaw's play *Man and Superman*, while Octave is the name of the protagonist of a Stendhal novel. And Octavius is the name of an old Roman general in the movie *Night at the Museum*.

Attractive foreign versions include Ottavio and Octavio, as in the distinguished Mexican poet Octavio Paz. Octavio is also the name of several saints, including one who lived as a hermit in an elm tree.

Odin

Norse, "fury"

Odin is the name of the supreme Norse god of art, culture, wisdom and law who was handsome, charming and eloquent into the bargain. The name projects a good measure of strength and power and has excellent assimilation potential. Could it make a possible alternative to Aiden?

The god Odin was referred to by more than 200 names, including Yggr, Sigfodr and Alfodr — none of which is recommended. The word Wednesday is derived from Woden, the English form of Odin.

Odin came to be used as a Norwegian male given name beginning in the nineteenth century, originally in the context of a romantic Viking revival. In the 2001 novel *American Gods* by Neil Gaiman; the character called Wednesday is an incarnation of the god Odin.

Oliver

Latin, "olive tree"

Oliver, now the Number 2 name in England, also entered the Top 100 in the U.S. for the first time in 2009, and is now at Number 73. Why? Because Oliver is energetic and good-natured, stylish but not nearly as trendy as twin-sister Olivia, with a meaning symbolizing peace and fruitfulness.

Oliver works particularly well with single-syllable surnames, as in Oliver Stone, North, and Puck (son of Wolfgang). Other celebrities who have chosen Oliver include Bridget Fonda, Julie Bowen, Fred Savage, Stephen Stills, and Taylor Hawkes.

Popular in medieval times, Oliver lost favor in England after the seventeenth-century rule of Oliver Cromwell, then was revived in the nineteenth century. Its biggest boost in this country came from the hit book and movie *Love Story*, which also catapulted Jennifer to stardom. Notable namesakes range from Oliver Wendell Holmes to Oliver Hardy to Oliver Stone. In fiction, there is Oliver Twist, and Oliver is also a *Harry Potter* name.

Oliver is enjoying huge popularity throughout Scandinavia at the moment, ranking Number 6 in Norway. More exotic foreign flair comes from the French Olivier, the Spanish Olivero and the Italian Oliviero.

Omar

Arabic, "flourishing, thriving"; Hebrew, "eloquent"

Omar has a perfect mix of exoticism and familiarity, with the additional plus of a strong, open initial "O." Commonly used among Muslim families, Omar was long associated with twelfth-century Persian poet Omar Khayyam, though it sounds anything but ancient now.

More recent well known bearers have been World War II General Omar Bradley and actors Omar Sharif (born Michael) and Omar Epps, and was a major character in *The Wire*.

Omar is also mentioned in the Old Testament book of Genesis. It has been in the US Top 200 since 1976.

Orion

Greek mythology name

Orion is a rising star, with both mythical and celestial overtones. Heard sporadically in the late nineteenth century, it burst on the US scene in full force in 1994 and has been shooting upwards ever since: it's now at Number 419.

The Greek mythological Orion was the legendary hunter who pursued the seven daughters of Atlas, was slain by the goddess Artemis, and then placed as one of the brightest constellations in the night sky by Zeus.

Mark Twain had a brother named Orion, and Chris "Big" Noth picked the name for his son. It is also a *Harry Potter* name.

Orion's Gaelic connection to O'Ryan/Ryan makes it familiar as well as exotic.

Orlando

Italian variation of Roland, "famous throughout the land"

Orlando, the ornate Italianate twist on the dated Roland, with a literary heritage stretching back to Shakespeare and before, has appealing book-ended "o"s, and is open to combination with almost any last name, a la British actor, Orlando Bloom.

Orlando has an impressive literary resume, including the poem "Orlando Furioso," Shakespeare's *As You Like It* and Virginia Woolf's enigmatic eponymous novel. Most recently, Orlando was a character in *The Wire*.

Orlando Bloom's name was inspired by that of the sixteenth-century composer, Orlando Gibbons. It is also the first name of several outstanding athletes — including Orlandos Woolridge, Cabrera, and Cepeda, and is, of course, a place name, home of Disney World in Florida.

Orson

Latin and English, "bear cub"

Orson has had in the past a rotund teddy-bear image, a la Orson Welles, who early on dropped his common given name of George in favor of his more distinctive middle one, and who seemed to own it during his lifetime. No longer a single-person signature, it's now an interesting possibility for any parent seeking an unusual yet solid name. It has started to appear to the celeb set — both Paz Vega and Lauren Ambrose have little Orsons.

The comic actor Orson Bean was born Dallas; there is a *Desperate Housewives* character called Orson Hodge.

There's also a fifteenth-century story about two brothers named Valentine and Orson, in which the latter was carried off by a bear and raised as one of its cubs.

Oscar

English, "God's spear," Irish, "deer-lover," or "champion warrior"

Oscar, a round and jovial choice, is a grandpa name that's fast taking over from such urban trendies as Max and Sam. Actors Hugh Jackman and Gillian Anderson chose Oscar for their sons.

In Irish legend, Oscar was one of the mightiest warriors of his generation, the son of Ossian and the grandson of Finn Mac Cumhaill (MacCool). In addition to being a Swedish royal name, Oscar has been especially popular with Latino families.

Famous Oscars include Wilde (whose given name was Fingal), Madison, Hammerstein, Peterson, de la Renta, the Academy Award, and the Grouch.

Oscar is currently the Number 2 name in Sweden.

Osias

Greek, "salvation"

Osias has a Latinate and biblical feel without making an appearance in the Bible. The related Ozias, on the other hand, is a form of Uzziah, found in the Greek and Latin Old Testament, and could make a distinctive path to the nickname Ozzie — both far cooler, in our opinion, than Oswald.

Otis

German, "wealthy"; variation of Otto

Otis has a double image: it's cool and bluesy a la Otis Redding, but also an upscale, high-society name of the past. Otis has real appeal for parents attracted to its catchy "O" initial and combination of strength and spunk.

Otis originally came into use as a tribute to the Revolutionary hero James Otis, and would be familiar to kids via the Disney film *The Adventures of Milo and Otis*.

Though well used at the turn of the last century, Otis has been off the charts since 1995, and now sounds like a fresh choice.

Otto

German, "wealthy"

Some truly cutting-edge parent might consider this German classic a so-far-out-it-could-come-back-in name à la Oscar: a nice round palindrome.

Like most German names, Otto fell out of favor during and after the two World Wars — it had been a Top 100 name in the years preceding. And there were some distinguished Ottos before the imperial image of Prussian Otto von Bismark colored the name. Otto the Great is generally considered the founder of the Holy Roman Empire and there were several German and Austrian royals with the name.

Othello is actually a diminutive of Otto.

Owen

Welsh, "young warrior; well-born"

Owen, a resonant Celtic name, has jumped almost three hundred places in a decade, with every indication it will go higher. Why do so many parents love Owen? It's a classic with a genuine history, yet it's right in step with the modern trend for two-syllable, "n" ending boys' names. Owen-like choices with less tradition behind them include Logan, Bowen, and Rowan.

The legendary St. Owen was a Benedictine monk who was a follower of St. Chad.

Owen is hot in Hollywood, picked by such stars as Phoebe Cates and Kevin Kline, Ricki Lake, and Noah Wyle.

In Ireland, Owen may be spelled Eoin, certain to be hugely confusing in the U.S., or Eoghan. Other similar names include the Scottish Ewan or Euan and the French Ouen.

Full disclosure: One of us has a son named Owen, who loves his name.

P

Painter

Occupational name

Painter is among the most creative choices in this very fashionable category of names, with a particularly pleasant sound. Whereas most occupational names conjure up physical labor, this one feels like a gateway to the arts.

Actor Chad Lowe used it as the middle name of his daughter Mabel.

Paolo

Italian variation of Paul, "small"

Paolo is an irresistibly lush name, worlds more romantic than its spare English equivalent.

Among noted bearers of the name are Renaissance painters Uccello and Veronese, architect Soleri, and whole teams of Italian soccer players — or so it seems.

Another possibility is the Spanish version of Paul: Pablo, as in Picasso and Casals.

Pascal

French, "of the Passover"; English, "Easter"

The French-accented Pascal was historically used for sons born at Easter, and can make an interesting choice for a boy with Gallic roots arriving around that holiday.

Pascal has a number of notable first and last named namesakes, including the philosopher Blaise Pascal, a character in *Beauty and the Beast* and — for computer freaks — it is also the name of a scientific database.

Pascoe is an attractive Cornish variation.

Patrick

Latin, "noble, patrician"

Patrick, long tied to a hyper-Irish image, is enjoying something of a renaissance as a stylish classic, which it has long been considered in England. Along with such choices as Charles and George, Patrick has escaped overuse in recent decades.

Though it's still at a healthy Number 142, why has Patrick slipped from its high of Number 30 in the 1960s? Partly to blame might be its androgynous nicknames, Pat and Patsy. But with more and more parents calling their sons by their full names, this becomes less of an issue. Patrick is still a Top 25 name in Ireland.

An American hero name via Patrick ("Give me liberty or give me death.") Henry, there are also a number of more recent noteworthy Patricks, including Ewing, Swayze, Dempsey, Buchanan, Stewart and Wilson. And Patrick is still a presence on such recent shows as *The Mentalist* and *Desperate Housewives*.

You also may want to consider the name's native version, Padraig, which was used for his son by Patrick Ewing, or a European form such as Patrice (French), Patrizio (Italian) or Patricio (Spanish).

Saint Patrick is the patron saint of Ireland, credited with converting his people to Christianity in the fifth century, which would give a son with this name a widely — and raucously — celebrated holiday.

Pax

Latin, "peaceful"
Pax, one of the variations of names meaning peace that are newly popular in these less-than-peaceful times, got a lot of publicity when chosen by Brad & Angelina for their Vietnamese-born son. Parents attracted to Pax may also want to consider Paz, the unisex Spanish version, or Paxton, a growing-in-popularity surname choice that shares that magical "x"-factor.

Paxton

Latin and English, "peace town"
Paxton stands out from a lot of other two-syllable surname names for two reasons: the dynamic letter "x" in the middle, and its admirable peace association, providing the great nickname Pax.

Paxton has risen from Number 420 to Number 241 in the past four years, making it one of the fastest-rising names for boys, while remaining a distinctive choice.

One well known bearer is the British actor Paxton Whitehead.

Penn

English, "enclosure"
This simple, elegant name offers something for many kinds of parents, from writers and history buffs to photographers to Pennsylvania dwellers. Most famous bearers are comedian Penn Jillette and *Gossip Girl* hottie Penn Badgley, both of whom were given this distinctive name at birth. Long obscure, Penn seems destined for greater usage.

More familiar as a surname, Penn has had a number of distinguished bearers, including Pennsylvania founder William, director Arthur, photographer Irving, and actor/activist Sean.

Percival

French, "one who pierces the valley"

There are several Percivals scattered through the *Harry Potter* series, which might help transform the old-fangled, effete image it has accrued. Actually, the original Percival was the one perfectly pure Knight of the Round Table, a worthy hero. The name was invented in the twelfth century by a poet named Chretien de Troyes, for his ideal knight in the poem *Percevale, a Knight of King Arthur*.

Percival is found in other forms of literature as well, including Wilkie Collins's *The Woman in White*, and Tennyson's *Idylls of the King* contains a section devoted to Sir Percival. Wagner transformed the name to Parsifal for his opera.

Percy, which seems like a nickname for Percival but is really a stand-alone Norman place name, is beginning to attract some favorable attention from cutting-edge namers.

Percy

French surname from place name Perci-en-Auge

Percy is an adorable old name that is finally shedding its prissy image in this new era of boys with soft yet traditionally male names like Jasper and Elijah. Originating as an aristocratic Norman name, Percy became fairly widespread in England — and to some extent in the U.S. — as an offshoot of the fame of the poet Percy Bysshe Shelley.

Percy Bresnahan is a character in the Sinclair Lewis novel *Main Street*, and one of Thomas the Tank Engine's sidekicks is named Percy.

Peregrine

Latin, "traveler, pilgrim"

Peregrine, considered to be an elegantly aristocratic name in England, has never made it to the U.S., where it tends to have been seen as extravagantly eccentric. In the new naming climate, though, it's not beyond consideration — in fact it's already been chosen by at least one Berry.

The meaning of Peregrine, which was borne by several early saints, relates to the transitory nature of life on earth, having nothing to do with the peregrine falcon. In literature, it is best known from the central character of Tobias Smollett's novel *Peregrine Pickle*.

Historically, Peregrine was the name chosen for the first English child born in the New World — actually on board the Mayflower when it was docked in Provincetown.

And there's always the *Mad Men*-era nickname Perry to make Peregrine more user-friendly.

Perry

English, "dweller near a pear tree"

It's a long time now since this casual but suave name was linked to velvet-throated, cardigan-sweatered singer Perry (born Pierino, son of Pietro) Como's day...and this could be the moment for a reassessment.

Another namesake is the fictional lawyer-detective created by Erle Stanley Gardner and later seen on TV, Perry Mason. There is also the option of taking the long way round to Perry via the more substantial Peregrine or Percival.

Perry/Peri is also occasionally used for girls.

Phelan

Irish, "wolf"

Phelan, pronounced FAY-lan or FEE-lan, is an appealing Irish surname name, with a rich history in Irish myth and religious and secular life. One bearer was a fiercely loyal follower of the legendary warrior Finn MacCool, another was a missionary saint.

The first name Phelan figures in an O'Henry story, *Between Rounds*; and in *The Help*, Skeeter's surname is Phelan. In Irish, the name is spelled Faolan.

Philip

Greek, "lover of horses"

Philip, the name of one of the twelve apostles, is still favored by parents in search of a solid boys' classic that is less neutral than Robert or John and more distinctive than Daniel or Matthew and has many historic, royal ties.

Famous bearers include Saint Philip, one of the twelve Apostles, King Philip the Great, who was the father of Alexander the Great, plus there have been numerous other French and Spanish rulers named Philip.

Thanks to the Duke of Edinburgh, though, Philip has a certain built-in reserve, somewhat straight and staid.

When it comes to nicknames, you're not limited to the mid-century Phil — more lively ones include Pip and Flip.

Model Eva Herzigova named her baby Philip — which can also be spelled Phillip, which is, in fact, the preferred spelling, ranking 59 places higher.

Some other modern Philip namesakes are writer Roth, actor Philip Seymour Hoffman, architect Johnson and composer Glass.

Philip comes via Latin from the Greek and was a name Top 100 choice for a century, before fading in the 1980s. In literature, Philip Pirrip is the full name of Pip from *Great Expectations*, and other Philips appear in the novels of Jane Austen, George Eliot and Thackeray — not to mention Raymond Chandler's detective Philip Marlowe.

Philo

Greek, "loving"

Could Philo be the next Milo? We love the "o" ending and sweet meaning of this dynamic and distinctive Greek name, often used in literature, but never particularly popular.

The ancient Philo (aka Philo of Alexandria and Philo the Jew) was a biblical philosopher who attempted to merge Greek and Jewish thought.

A character named Philo was a minor figure in Shakespeare's *Antony and Cleopatra*, it was the name of the S. S. Van Dine aristocratic dandy detective Philo Vance, and Clint Eastwood's character in both *Any Which Way You Can* and *Any Which Way But Loose* was Philo Beddoe. Most well-known Philo is real life was inventor Philo Farnsworth.

Phineas

Hebrew, "oracle"

Julia Roberts drew the biblical Phineas into the limelight when she chose it, with the even-more-antique spelling Phinnaeus, for her twin son, now called Finn. Phineas had last been heard from via circus impresario Phineas T. Barnum, until it was brought somewhat up to date via the Disney Channel animated show *Phineas and Ferb*.

Anthony Trollope combined name and nickname for the young, handsome and charming Irish lawyer hero of his eponymous novel, *Phineas Finn*. Phineas is also the name of three biblical personages and was popular among the seventeenth-century Puritans. Jazz pianist Phineas Newborn, Jr is a contemporary namesake.

Trivia note: In early movies, characters named Phineas had nicknames like Prune, Whipsnake, and Whoopee.

Bottom line: A quirky path to nickname Finn.

Piers

Greek, "rock"

Piers was the first version of Peter to reach the English-speaking world, via the Normans, but it's never made it in the U.S., despite its large measure of understated panache. This might change due to the high visibility of TV personality and former news editor Piers Morgan.

There's a famous satirical medieval poem called *Piers Plowman*, in which the title character symbolizes the virtues of honesty and industry. Piers Whiteoak is a main character in the sixteen-book series *Jalna* by Canadian author Mazo de la Roche; Piers Polkiss is the best friend of Harry's cousin Dudley in the *Harry Potter* books.

The surname form of the name, Pierce, is better known in the U.S., partly via actor Pierce Brosnan.

Pike

Animal name

The field of nature names is constantly expanding to include all species of flowers and trees and animals and birds — and even fish. In addition to its appeal for anglers, Pike recalls Zebulon Pike, the explorer who discovered and gave his name to Pike's Peak.

While Pike also shares the friendly feel of names like Mike and Ike, the word pike can also be a noun or verb referring to a long sharp weapon used to do not-very-friendly things to people.

Plato

Greek, "broad-shouldered"

The name of one of the greatest Western philosophers is often used as a first name in its land of origin, Greece, and would make a really interesting, thought-provoking choice here. It is remembered here as the nickname of the memorable character played by Sal Mineo in the classic film *Rebel Without a Cause*.

And speaking of Greek philosophers, Germaine Clement of *Flight of the Conchords* named his little boy Sophocles.

Poe

English, "peacock"

An evocative unisex one-syllable name, Poe is most distinguished by its literary reference. Edgar Allan Poe was an influential American author and poet, credited with inventing the genres of detective and science fiction, which might provide inspiration for parents who are fans.

The female singer-songwriter professionally known as Poe was born with the more prosaic name Ann.

The variant spelling Po is identified with Po Bronson, the chronicler of the technological age, and also has the geographical association with the river in northern Italy.

Prescott

English, "priest's cottage"

Prescott is one of several distinguished, upper-crusty surnames beginning with "P."

There are several historical surnamed Prescotts, including William, a Massachusetts Minuteman and commander at the battle of Bunker Hill, and Samuel, a Revolutionary patriot who traveled with Paul Revere on the night of his famous ride. Prescott is also the first name of the father and brother of George H.W. Bush.

Preston

English, "priest's estate"

Britney Spears put this old-fashioned surname name back on the map when she chose it as her son Sean's middle name, which the family uses as his first.

One of the most popular names of its genre, Preston is now at Number 129, having been in the Top 200 since 1994. It's been heard on such TV shows as *Desperate Housewives*, *Grey's Anatomy*, and *The Wire*. The most memorable bearer of the name is probably Preston Sturges (born Edmund), one of the leading screwball comedy writer/directors of Hollywood's Golden Age.

Primo

Italian, "first"

Primo is Number 1 among the Latin birth-order names — Octavius et al — and the one most likely to be used in these days of smaller families. It has that jaunty "o" ending and Italian flavor that many modern parents like so much. And what little boy wouldn't appreciate being prime?

Italian author Primo Levi, known for his writings on the Holocaust, is a famous bearer.

Prosper

Latin, "favorable, prosperous"

In France, pronounced PRO-spare, Prosper is a fairly common name; here it presents a worthy aspirational message for a child.

Prosper was the name of several early saints, including a noted fifth-century theologian, St. Prosper of Aquitaine, and was a favorite of English Puritans.

Prosper has strong associations with P. Mérimée, who wrote the novel *Carmen*, upon which the opera is based. Prospers were also the protagonists of two other books, *The Shining Company* by Rosemary Sutcliff and *The Thief Lord* by Cornelia Funke.

The Italian version, Prospero, is another attractive option, with ties to Shakespeare's magician character in "The Tempest."

Q

Quade

Latin, "fourth" or "born fourth"

Quade is a confident, contemporary-sounding name that would fit right in with classmates Cade, Zade, Slade and Jade, boasting the quirky "Q" beginning.

Quade Cooper is an Australian rugby star. With the alternate spelling Quaid, the name is associated with thespian brothers Dennis and Randy.

Quentin

Latin, "fifth"

Quentin, an offbeat name with lots of character, relates to the Latin for the number five and is by far the most subtle and most usable of the Latin birth-order names, masculine as well as stylish and distinctive.

Sir Walter Scott wrote the novel *Quentin Durward* in 1823, about a young, upper-class Scotsman, and Quentin Compson is both a male and a female character in William Faulkner's *The Sound and the Fury*. Real life bearers include cutting-edge movie director Quentin Tarantino, eccentric British author Quentin Crisp, and Quentin Blake, illustrator of Roald Dahl books.

Quentin is currently a Top 40 name in France.

Trivia tidbit: St. Quentin is the protector against coughs.

Quincy

French, "estate of the fifth son"

Quirky in the way that all Q names are quirky, Quincy was once a buttoned-up, patrician New England name, an image countered in recent years by the talented and ultracool musician Quincy Jones (middle name: Delight; nickname: Q).

The middle name of John Quincy Adams, the sixth U.S. President, who was named for his mother's maternal grandfather, Colonel John Quincy, after whom Quincy, Massachusetts, is named.

Quinn

Irish, "descendant of Conn, chief leader, intelligence"

Quinn is an engaging Celtic surname that is on the rise for both genders. Though still used more for boys, Quinn has started leaning decidedly toward the feminine thanks to a female cheerleader character on the television show *Glee*. It retains some testosterone from *The Mighty Quinn,* the name of a movie, a band, and a Bob Dylan song.

Sharon Stone has a son named Quinn. Other ideas for boyish names like Quinn: Quinton, Quincy, Finn.

R

Rafferty

Irish, "floodtide, abundance, prosperity"

Jaunty and raffish, Rafferty is one of the most engaging of the Irish surnames, used by Jude Law and Sadie Frost for their son. Fortunately, it doesn't still go by its original form: O'Raighbheartaigh.

Raff and Rafe are two equally great nicknames.

Ralph

English from German, "wolf-counsel"

Ralph has two diametrically different images: there's the suave Ralph Fiennes-type Brit (often pronounced Rafe), and then there's the Jackie Gleason blue-collar, bowling blowhard Ralph Kramden bus driver. It's all in the eye of the beholder, though Ralph's hip factor did rise when it was chosen for his son by cool U.K. actor Matthew Macfadyen.

Ralph is a name that's been around for a thousand years, was in the Top 30 from the 1870s to the 1920s, and just could make a comeback.

Ralph has a number of notable namesakes, from Ralph Waldo Emerson to Ralph Abernathy to Ralph Lauren. In literature, Ralph is a Shakespearean name, appearing in *Henry IV*, is a pivotal figure in Henry James's *The Portrait of a Lady* and Ralph was one of the three main boys in *Lord of the Flies*. And let's not forget Ralphie in *A Christmas Story*.

Or you might prefer the French version — Raoul.

Ranger

French, "forest guardian"

The list of occupational boys' names continues to expand, and this is one of the latest to ride onto the range. And, as trends collide, it also has the popular western, cowboyish feel. A much better choice than the increasingly (and scarily) heard Danger.

Raphael

Hebrew, "God has healed"

Raphael is a romantic archangel name that sounds both artistic and powerful. Raphael is also a great cross-cultural choice, with significance for people with both Latinate and Jewish roots, plus plenty of grounding in the English-speaking world.

Raphael was one of the seven archangels (called by Milton "the affable archangel") who attended the throne of God and, as the angel of healing, is the patron of doctors as well as of travelers, science, and healing. Another worthy namesake is the great Renaissance painter Raphael (born Raffaello Sanzio).

Raphael is particularly popular in France right now, where it's a Top 10 name. Rafael is the Spanish spelling, as represented by Spanish tennis champ Rafael Nadal. Rafi is the familiar Hebrew nickname.

Ray

Diminutive of Raymond, "wise protector"

Ray, still and forever, is one of the all-time hippest names, with its jazzy Ray Charles biopic overtones. It makes a cool middle name (as Rae does for girls), but works perfectly fine as a first.

The list of noteworthy Rays who have brought glory to their nickname name goes on forever — Bradbury, Romano, Milland (born Alfred), Liotta, and Goulding, to name just a few.

Raymond

German, "wise-protector"

Now that the show has gone into reruns, does anybody still love Raymond? Though it's been long dormant, some parents — including Jack Nicholson — are finding its cool component, largely through the nickname Ray.

Raymond was introduced into England by the Normans and was a favorite in the time of the Crusades.

Raymond was a Top 20 name in 1900, and continued to be popular through the era of Raymond Chandler and Raymond Burr and Raymond Massey. More recently there was the eminent short story writer Raymond Carver.

Bottom line: Raymond hasn't quite crossed into Clunky Cool territory yet, but he might just follow his own nickname there.

Redmond

Irish variation of Raymond, "wise protector"

We love this partly for purely personal reasons, since it is one of our surnames. We used it as the middle name of a son — and it can make a good first choice too.

Redmond — aka Reamann or Raemonn — is the Irish form of the Germanic name that occurs in modern English as Raymond. One seventeenth-century Redmond O'Hanlon was a charismatic outlaw, and he has a modern namesake who is a well-known travel writer.

In Ireland, Mundy is sometimes used as a nickname.

Reed

English, "red-haired"

A slim, elegant, silvery surname, Reed could be a banker or a sculptor, and therein lays the appeal of this simple yet distinctive name.

The versatile Reed can be seen as a grass-like nature name and a musical name.

There have been Reeds on *Grey's Anatomy* and *Party of 5*, and on the big screen in *Boogie Nights*. Reed Richards was the human name of the scientific genius who became Mister Fantastic of the Fantastic Four.

The many notables who wore Reed as a surname include army surgeon Walter, basketball coach Willis, *Brady Bunch* dad Robert, critic Rex, director Sir Carol, actors Donna and Oliver, and singer-songwriter Lou.

The name can also be spelled Reid, which ranks higher in the popularity standings.

Reeve

English occupational name, "bailiff"

Reeve is cool and dignified, sophisticated and modern — an excellent combination of assets, and a name being seen as a more masculine and distinctive alternative to Reese.

A reeve was a medieval English manor officer responsible for overseeing the discharge of feudal obligations. Reeve has very occasionally been used for girls: it was the name of the daughter of Charles and Anne Morrow Lindbergh, their youngest child.

Remy

French from Latin, "oarsman"

The name of a fifth-century saint, Remy sounds particularly modern and attractive and is being revived for both boys and girls, sometimes as Remi. It entered the popularity list in 2009, and jumped almost 100 places the following year.

Remy came into the spotlight via the 2007 Disney film *Ratatouille*, "starring an ambitious chef named Remy — who happened to be a rat. The name has also been borne by a variety of human characters in *The Da Vinci Code*, *House*, *New Girl*, and *The Fairly Oddparents*.

Remy de Gourmont was a French Symbolist poet, Remy Charlip a children's book author and illustrator.

Reuben

Hebrew, "behold, a son"

Reuben is a rich and resonant underused Old Testament choice with several ingredients for success: its biblical pedigree as Jacob's first-born son by Leah and the founder of one of the tribes of Israel, the distinction of never having been heavily used, and a friendly, down-home image. Maybe the current crowd of Jacobs will grow up and follow their biblical namesake by calling their own sons Reuben.

Only downsides: Reuben is also known as a sandwich, and is the source of the word "rube" — and logical nickname Ruby is feminine.

Panama-born salsa singer Ruben Blades represents the Latin version (with the accent on the second syllable); Reuven is the name in Hebrew.

Rex

Latin, "king"

Now that many dogs are named Max, it's safe to use this sleek, sexy, regal name again for your child. And with the charm of its final "x," its regal meaning and its offbeat simplicity, Rex is definitely one to consider.

Coldplay's Will Champion used it for his twin son, and Natascha McElhone gave her little boy the doubly cool appellation Rex Coltrane, while Niki Taylor — intentionally or not — gave her son the full name of the British My Fair Lady star, Rex Harrison. Rex ("Sexy Rexy") Harrison was actually christened Reginald.

Other options: the French version Regis or the literal King.

Reynard

German, "powerful advice"

Associated with Reynard the cunning fox in medieval European animal tales. Reynard can make an unusual yet historic choice for a modern boy, a modern day Richard or Robert.

Rhett

English from Dutch, "advice"

Rhett has been more tied to *Gone with the Wind* than even Scarlett, but now we're hearing rumblings of its finding new and independent favor among parents, perhaps emboldened by the growing popularity of Scarlett. Rhett is more popular today than it's ever been.

In addition to being a powerful storyteller, author Margaret Mitchell was a great character namer as well — think Scarlett, Melanie, Ashley, and even the mansion Tara. Rhett emerged from the story as one of the ultimate dashing, romantic names — so much so that parents of the past didn't fully embrace it.

Rhett is a South Carolina surname, brought to North America in 1694, and borne by a noted politician during the Civil War period, which may have inspired the author.

Rhys

Welsh, "ardor"

There's Rhys and there's Reese (now more popular for girls) and there's Reece, and we particularly like the traditional Welsh spelling, which has been climbing since it entered the list in 2004, possibly influenced by Jonathan Rhys Meyers, of *The Tudors*, and Welsh-born actor Rhys Ifans.

Always widespread in Wales, where it has deep historic roots, Rhys is also a Top 70 name in England, Ireland and Scotland.

Former New Kid on the Block Joey McIntyre named his son Rhys Edward in 2009.

Rio

Spanish, "river"; Brazilian place-name

Rio is a reductive ranchero place-name with an attractive Tex-Mex lilt. No Doubt's Tom Dumont has a son named Rio Atticus.

Also a South American place name, and associated with the Rio Grande, it's been used as a swaggering cowboy name in films spanning from a William S. Hart character in 1915 to Marlon Brando's in *One-Eyed Jacks*. It is occasionally used for a girl, as in the catchy Duran Duran song.

River

Nature name

River shares the tranquil feeling of all the water names, and seems to have pretty much escaped its past strong association with River Phoenix and his unfortunate fate. Keri Russell and the

Taylor Hansons both have sons named River, Natasha Henstridge used it as the middle name of her boy Tristan, and Jason Schwartzman pluralized it for daughter Marlowe Rivers.

One of the leading nature names, River now ranks at Number 407. About two-thirds of the babies named River these days are boys.

Rocco

Italian from German, "rest"

Madonna did much to polish up the image of this old-neighborhood Italian choice when she picked it for her son with British director Guy Ritchie; it now feels much more mainstream, sharing the quirky appeal of some other so-far-out-they're-in names as Bruno and Hugo.

Legendary boxers Rocky Graziano and Rocky Marciano were both born Rocco. Rocco DiSpirito is an award-winning celebrity chef; Rocco Landesman is a noted Broadway producer.

Rollo

Latin form of Rolf, "wolf"

Rollo is a livelier, roly-poly, "o" ending version of Roland.

Although it sounds modern, Rollo actually was seen regularly on Latin documents in the Middle Ages, though not heard in everyday speech. Historically, it's associated with a powerful Viking leader — who had a wife named Poppa.

Rollo May was a well-known existential psychologist. There have been Rollos on screen played by Buster Keaton (*The Navigator*), Rainn Wilson (*Juno*) and John Cleese (*Fierce Creatures*).

Rollo has also been used over the years as a pet form of Roland, Rudolph and Ralph.

Roman

Latin, "citizen of Rome"

Roman — a surprise hit name of recent years — owes much of its popularity to Cate Blanchett and Debra Messing, who almost simultaneously chose Roman for their sons, as Molly Ringwald did later.

In fact, several relatives of Roman are also newly stylish, from Romy to Romilly to Romeo. Definitely a romantic name, however you use it. This year, Roman sits at Number 159.

Well-known Romans include director Polanski (born Raimund), Polish photographer Vishniac, and onetime star quarterback Gabriel. Francis Ford Coppola has a son named Roman, who is a director now himself.

The French version is Romaine — and literary parents might appreciate the fact that "roman" is the French word for novel.

Romeo

Italian, "pilgrim to Rome, Roman"

It wasn't so long ago that Romeo was considered as outré for an American baby as Casanova or Cupid. But that really changed when David and Victoria Beckham chose it for their second son in 2002, a path followed by Jon Bon Jovi. The most romantic of Shakespearean male names, Romeo shot up more than fifty places from 2009 to 2010, and now rests at 323.

Romeo was not invented by the Bard, but was taken from his source material for the play. Some sources say it descends from that of Romulus, one of the twin sons of Mars.

Ronan

Irish, "little seal"

Ronan is the compelling legendary name of twelve Irish and Scottish saints that is now drawing some deserved attention; this cousin of the ascending Roman and Rowan was chosen by actor Daniel Day-Lewis and his writer-director wife Rebecca Miller in 1998, and more recently by actress Catherine Bell.

Now ranking Number 456 in the U.S., Ronan is, not surprisingly, a Top 50 name in Ireland and Number 52 in Northern Ireland. Ronan is a *Harry Potter* name — that of a centaur who lives in the Forbidden Forest; Ronan Keating is an Irish singer, and its presence as a surname is represented by young actress Saoirse Ronan.

Roone

Irish, "red-haired"

Roone is a lively, attractive and unusual redhead entry brought into the mix by the late TV sports and news executive Roone Arledge, who seemed to own it as a one-person name when he was alive.

Roone can also be seen/used as a short form of Rooney.

Rory

Irish, "red king"

This spirited Gaelic classic, which became popular in Ireland via the illustrious twelfth-century king Rory O'Connor, makes a highly energetic choice, now used for either sex. Rory's gender split is trending boyward: 58% of the children named Rory in the most recent year counted were boys and 42% girls, compared with a near-even split just a few years ago.

Rory first came to attention in the U.S. in the person of mid-century pin-up boy, Rory Calhoun (born Francis Timothy); the name entered the popularity list in 1947, peaking at Number 280 in 1959.

Young Irish U.S. Open champ Rory McIlroy makes a worthy namesake. Bill and Melinda Gates chose Rory as the name of their only son.

Rory is a Top 40 name in Scotland and is also well used in Ireland. Skip baffling Gaelic spellings like Ruari and Ruaidhri and stick with the more straightforward Rory.

Roscoe

Norse, "deer forest"

Fairly popular a hundred years ago but out of sight now, the quirky Roscoe deserves a place on every adventurous baby-namer's long list. It joins Rufus, Roman, Remy, Romulus, and Ray as one of the "R" names that sound fresh again after too many years of Robert, Richard, and Ronald.

Originally a place and surname, Roscoe had its glory days in the 1880s, when it reached as high as Number 138, then gradually declined, possibly damaged by the scandals surrounding silent star Roscoe "Fatty" Arbuckle, and then the hillbilly image it acquired thanks to Sheriff Coltrane on *The Dukes of Hazzard*. Roscoe has been out of the Top 1000 since 1978.

Trivia tidbit: The R in Edward R. Murrow stands for Roscoe; the distinguished newsman's first name was really Egbert.

Rowan

Scottish and Irish, "little redhead"

Rowan — a strong surname and nature name (it's a tree with red berries) — is deservedly growing in popularity. Some scholars identify Rowan as originally a girl's name, related to Rowena and Rhonwen, while others say Rowan's always been used for both genders. Sharon Stone chose the Roan spelling, which also relates to the reddish color, for her son, while Brooke Shields used Rowan for her daughter. Rowen is yet another spelling growing in popularity.

Probably the most prominent bearer of the name is Rowan Atkinson, the British comic actor first seen on the sitcom *Blackadder*, but even better known for his Mr. Bean persona.

Roy

French, "king," Celtic, "red-haired"

We've seen Ray regain his cool, but could this country/cowboy name epitomized by Roys Rogers (born Leonard Slye), Acuff, and Clark, do the same?

Roy came into use in the late nineteenth century, probably influenced by the main character of Sir Walter Scott's novel *Rob Roy*, in which the historical character Robert MacGregor is nicknamed Roy for his red hair.

There have been lots of notable non-country namesakes, including baseball's Roy Campanella, humorist Roy Blunt, Jr, Walt's brother and partner Roy Disney, singer Roy Orbison and pop artist Roy Lichtenstein. Roy Hobbs was the protagonist of the Malamud novel *The Natural*, played in the film by Robert Redford.

Roy was also the first name of clothing designer Halston.

Rudy

German, short form of Rudolph, "famous wolf"

Rudy hasn't yet enjoyed the comeback of girl cousin name Ruby, despite having been chosen by hip couple Sadie Frost and Jude Law, but it still could happen.

Rudy has a lot going for it as a usable-on-its-own nickname name, with the lively "oo" sound found in Jude and Juno and all the popular "Lu"-starting names. And it was a heartthrob name back in the day when crooner Rudy (born Hubert) Vallee and Rudy/Rudolph (born Rodolpho) Valentino had ladies swooning, reaching as high as Number 299 in 1926.

It has most often been seen as an all-male name — except for little Rudy on *The Cosby Show*.

Rufus

Latin, "red-head"

Rufus is a rumpled, redheaded (it was the nickname for red-haired King William) ancient Roman name popular with saints and singers (e.g. Rufus Wainwright); now, Rufus is on the cutting edge of cool.

Fellow singer James Taylor named one of his twins Rufus, and Rufus Humphrey is a *Gossip Girl* character. Rufus Sewell is a commanding, intense English actor.

Rufus is mentioned in the New Testament as the name of a son of Simon the Cytherian, and there are several St. Rufuses. He's also a major figure in the George Eliot novel *Felix Holt: The Radical*, an honest and passionate preacher and politician.

Rupert

German variation of Robert, "bright fame"

Rupert is a charming-yet-manly name long more popular in Britain (where it's attached to a beloved cartoon bear) than in the U.S. Yet we can see Rupert as a more stylish, modern way to honor an ancestral Robert.

Rupert has been more visible in this country of late via Rupert Grint, portrayer of *Harry Potter*'s Ron Weasley and the character Rupert Giles, mentor of Buffy in *Buffy the Vampire Slayer*, as well as actors Rupert Everett and Rupert Graves — not to mention media mogul Rupert Murdoch.

Ryder

British surname, "cavalryman, messenger"

Ryder, one of the current favorite "er" ending boys' names, has been in the spotlight since Kate Hudson and her rocker husband Chris Robinson chose it for their son in 2004; it has jumped nearly seven hundred places in the past decade, now at a high Number 100. Very popular in several provinces of Canada, Ryder was also chosen by John Leguizamo for his son.

In the past, Ryder was much more prevalent as a surname, as in American Old Master painter Albert Pinkham Ryder and *Brideshead Revisited* protagonist Charles Ryder. Not all came by it legitimately, however — Winona Ryder was born Winona Horowitz.

Trivia note: The Ryder Cup is a biennial golf tournament with competing teams from Europe and the U.S.

S

Samson

Hebrew, "sun"

With the prevailing popularity of Samuel, some parents are considering this more (literally) powerful biblical name, which shares the desirable nickname of Sam.

Samson was, of course, the supernaturally strong champion of the Israelites against the Philistines who was betrayed by Delilah, as dramatized in more than one Technicolor epic. But the more it is used for children today, the more the name is able to move away from that image.

Sampson is a variant spelling — Sampson Brass is a character in the Dickens novel *The Old Curiosity Shop*, Samzun is the interesting Celtic spelling, Sansone the Italian version.

The story of Samson has been translated into a number of works of art, including Milton's poetic drama *Samson Agonistes*, an oratorio by Handel, an opera by Saint-Saens, and paintings by Rembrandt and Rubens.

Samuel

Hebrew, "told by God"

Samuel has long been a popular Old Testament classic, and is currently just inside the Top 25, with close to 11,000 boys named Samuel annually. Its continued use is somewhat propelled by the likability of the friendly nickname Sam, which returned to favor along with fellow former cigar-chomping movie moguls Max and Jake. Sam is now often used on its own, for girls as well as boys.

In the Old Testament, Samuel was one of the great judges and prophets of the Israelites, destined for a holy life from birth. He established the Hebrew monarchy, anointing both Saul and David as kings.

High-profile celebs who have chosen Samuel for their sons include Jennifer Garner and Ben Affleck, Jack Black, and Naomi Watts and Liev Schreiber.

Saul

Hebrew, "prayed for"

Jewish parents in particular may be drawn to this quiet, composed name of the first king of Israel and the name of Saint Paul before his conversion. In modern times, it has been associated with Nobel Prize-winning novelist Saul Bellow. Its meaning makes it appropriate for a long-awaited child.

Saul is a character in a John Dryden poem, and heard in the Handel oratorio, *Saul*.

Some other Sauls of note: Saul Steinberg, known for his iconic New Yorker covers, and graphic artist/movie credit designer Saul Bass. The birth name of Guns N' Roses's Slash is Saul Hudson.

Sawyer

English, "woodcutter"

Sawyer is a surname with a more relaxed and friendly feel than many others, and is one of the hottest occupational names right now, wearing the Nameberry seal of approval. Sawyer is becoming increasingly unisex — both Sara Gilbert and Diane Farr used Sawyer for their daughters — though it was also given a boost by *Lost*'s James Sawyer.

Kate Capshaw and Steven Spielberg were among the first to discover Sawyer when they used it for their son in 1992, the year it leaped up 356 places; it's now at Number 147. Sawyer recently entered the girls' Top 1000, ranking Number 548 in 2010.

Sawyer is a relatively common surname — think Tom and Diane.

Sayer

Welsh, "carpenter"

One of the more subtle occupational surnames, Sayer is a pleasant, open, last-name-first name, particularly apt for a family of woodworkers — or writers. Some parents are beginning to consider Sayer as a less-popular alternative to Sawyer.

The most well-known surnamed Sayer is the British singer Leo Sayer.

Seamus

Irish variation of James, "supplanter"

Parents who have tired of Sean are now contemplating Seamus, the Irish form of James, which has a lot more substance and verve.

One of the name's most famous bearers is the late 1995 Nobel Prize-winning Irish poet Seamus Heaney. Seamus is also a *Harry Potter* name — Seamus Finnigan being a half-blood wizard friend of Harry's.

At a time when the police force was predominantly Irish, "shamus" became a slang term for a detective.

Sebastian

Latin from Greek, "person from ancient city of Sebasta"

Sebastian is an ancient martyr's name turned literary, and *Little Mermaid* hero — think Sebastian the Crab — that's entered the Top 70 as a classic-yet-unconventional compatriot for fellow British favorites Colin and Oliver.

Sebastian is a name with a substantial history, first as the third-century martyr whose sufferings was a favorite subject of medieval artists, then as the name of memorable characters in such varied works as Shakespeare's *Twelfth Night* and *The Tempest* and Evelyn Waugh's *Brideshead Revisited*.

Several celebs have chosen the sophisticated Sebastian for their sons, including James Spader, Kim Fields, Malin Akerman and Tommy Hilfiger.

Sebastian is high on the lists in countries as widespread as Austria, Denmark, Romania, Australia and Chile. Some more down-to-earth nicknames for the relatively elaborate Sebastian not often heard in this country are Seb, Baz and Bas.

Septimus

Latin, "the seventh son"

Septimus is one of the more dashing of the birth-order Latin number names that were revived by the Victorians. So even if you don't anticipate son number 7, you might be bold enough to consider this relic, certainly preferable to sixth-son name Sextus.

Septimus was popularized by the Roman Emperor Septimus Severus, a patron of arts and letters. There was a Septimus in Wilkie Collins's *The Moonstone*, in Dickens's *The Mystery of Edwin Drood*, and in Trollope's *Barchester* novels. Probably it is most familiar to modern readers as one of the principal characters in Virginia Woolf's *Mrs. Dalloway*, and as *Harry Potter* wizard, Septimus Weasley. There is also *Septimus Heap*, a series of bestselling fantasy novels by Angie Sage.

Seth

Hebrew, "appointed, placed"

The long neglected name of Adam and Eve's third son, Seth is now being increasingly appreciated for its gentle, understated presence, and its strong middle-name potential.

Seth was widely heard in the American old West, as reflected in such vintage TV oaters as *Wagon Train*, featuring Major Seth Adams. George Eliot and Charles Dickens both created characters named Seth and there is a *Twilight* werewolf called Seth Clearwater.

Currently, Seth has taken on a lighter persona via such high-profile comical Seths as *SNL*'s Seth Meyers, the movies' Seth Rogen, and animated comedy creator Seth MacFarlane.

Shaw

English, "dweller by the wood"

With the current taste for last names first, this sounds a lot cooler than Shawn; it also has creative connections to the great Irish playwright, George Bernard Shaw, novelist Irwin Shaw, and Big Band Era clarinetist/bandleader and one-time Ava Gardner husband Artie Shaw.

Since Shaw has never appeared in the Top 1000, a boy given this name could really make it his own.

Shepherd

Occupational name

Shepherd is an occupational surname with a pleasant pastoral feel. It was chosen for their son by the Jerry Seinfelds, which might inspire others to follow their lead.

There are other spelling choices — Shepard, Sheperd, Sheppard — all of which lead to the friendly nickname Shep. Artist Shepard Fairey (original first name Frank) gained a lot of attention for his Obama HOPE poster.

Those various spellings are reflected in the surnames of such notables as astronaut Alan Shepard, *Winnie the Pooh* illustrator Ernest Shepard, actor/playwright Sam Shepard, *A Christmas Story* writer Jean Shepherd and actress Cybill Shepherd.

Silas

English from Latin, "wood"

Silas, once a folksy-sounding, rural New Testament name associated with George Eliot's *Silas Marner*, is definitely beginning to be reevaluated, à la similar flavored Caleb and Linus, and becoming a hot Nameberry fave.

Silas is also associated with the indelible albino monk in *The Da Vinci Code*, was the leading character in William D. Howell's novel *The Rise and Fall of Silas Lapham*, and was the name of Nancy Botwin's son in *Weeds*.

Silas is based on Sylvanus, the Roman god of trees and was originally bestowed on people who lived in wooded areas or who worked with wood.

In 2009 alone, Silas shot up more than 50 places, then 12 more in 2012, indicating that it is a rising New Testament name.

St. Silas was a leading member of the early Christian community who accompanied Paul on his second missionary journey.

Simeon

Hebrew, "God is listening"

Could Simeon be the next Gideon? Parents seeking a less-simple form of Simon might consider this biblical appellation that was chosen by Wynton Marsalis for his son. Simon is actually the Greek substitute for Simeon.

The first known Simeon was Leah and Jacob's son, who gave his name to one of the twelve tribes of Israel, the Simeonites; in the New Testament it is the name of the man who blessed the infant Christ. Both Simeon and Simon were popular names for saints. One caveat: Simeon is undeniably similar to the word meaning "apelike."

Simon

Hebrew, "the listener"

Simon is pure and simple (not in the nursery rhyme sense), and an appealingly genuine Old and New Testament name that's not overused — making it a stylish choice.

In the Bible, Simon was the second son of Jacob and Leah and the original name of Saint Peter, as well as the name of several New Testament figures. Historically, Simón Bolivar is known as The Liberator of South America.

Simon was one of the more appealing characters in *Lord of the Flies*, then became part of the British invasion of names that hit U.S. shores along with the Beatles. Other recent notable Simons include Simon Templar — aka The Saint, Simon Cowell, who became famous as the snarky judge on *The X Factor*, Simon Le Bon, lead singer of Duran, Duran, and Simon Baker, Australian-born star of *The Mentalist*.

Simon is currently very popular in several European countries, including Austria, Denmark, France, Sweden, Switzerland, and Belgium.

Sinjin

Phonetic spelling of St. John

The name St. John is much more usable and exotic in its phonetic spelling — similar to the way St. Clair evolved into Sinclair. St. John has some literary cred — St. John Rivers is a cool character in *Jane Eyre*.

St. John has been attached to a number of notable men — not as a first but as a middle name, one shared by Evelyn Waugh, Basil Rathbone, Richard Harris and Brian Eno.

Sky

Nature name

Sky is an ambigender nature name that was first legitimized as the character of Sky Masterson in the 1950 musical *Guys and Dolls*, played in the film version by Marlon Brando. It's a name we appreciate for its clear, wide-open feel, less hippyish than others like Rainbow and Starlight, and it makes an appealing middle name possibility.

Sky is the name of Sophie's fiancé in *Mamma Mia*, and there are both Power Rangers and Transformers with the name. Elizabeth Berkley used it for her son, David Copperfield for his daughter.

It is also spelled Skye, as in the island in the Inner Hebrides of Scotland. Plus, it's a logical nickname for the variously spelled Schuylers and Skylers.

Slade

English, "from the valley"

Evoking the image of a shady glen, Slade could make a distinctive middle name. It entered the Top 1000 in 2007, and has been seen as a character name on the TV show *Smallville*. It's also a name that pops up in comic books and video games.

Slater

English occupational name, "maker of slates"

Slater has a more genial, friendly feel than most trade names. Angela Bassett and Courtney B. Vance used it for one of their twins.

On the 90s TV show *Saved by the Bell*, the character A.C. Slater, played by Mario Lopez, was usually referred to by his surname. Christian Slater is a well-known real life bearer — though he was born Christian Hawkins.

Smith

English occupational name, "blacksmith"

Even if it is the Number 1 surname in the U.S. — with more than 2.5 million bearers — we still think that Smith would make a cool first or middle name, whether or not it has family history.

Though Smith was in fairly regular use until the 1920s — reaching as high as Number 326 in 1885 — it would make a totally distinctive, sophisticated choice today.

Solomon

Hebrew, "peace"

Solomon, a name that evokes wisdom and peace, is an Old Testament name that, along with other patriarchal classics, is finally beginning to shed its long white beard and step from the pages of the Old Testament into modern nurseries.

Originating from the Hebrew word "shalom," meaning peace, Solomon was a favorite of Charles Dickens, who used it for characters in three of his novels.

Solomon Grundy is a name that moved from a nursery rhyme ("Solomon Grundy, born on a Monday") to a DC Comics character to the name of a California rock group.

The biblical Solomon, the son of David and Bathsheba, succeeded his father as king of Israel, and was known for his wisdom ("People came from all the nations to hear the wisdom of Solomon."). He is credited with writing the biblical books Proverbs, Ecclesiastes and the Song of Solomon — the latter also the title of an acclaimed Toni Morrison novel.

Notable bearers of the name include philanthropist Solomon R. Guggenheim, for whom the New York museum is named, and singer-songwriter Solomon Burke, sometimes referred to as "King Solomon."

Soren

Danish and Norwegian variation of Severus, "stern"
This gentle Danish name, soft and sensitive, still has more masculine punch than the dated Loren. It's most closely identified with the nineteenth-century philosopher Søren Kierkegaard, but there have been modern fictional Sorens as well, in *The Matrix Reloaded* and the book series *Guardians of Ga'Hook*, *Charlie and Lola*, and *Underworld*.

Spencer

English, "house steward, dispenser of provisions"
Spencer is a name that has everything: it's both distinguished sounding and accessible, dignified but Spencer Tracy-like friendly. Picked by several celebrities (a couple of times even for a girl), all adding up to an enthusiastically recommended choice.

As a family surname, Spencer became the middle name of Winston Churchill, and was the maiden name of Princess Diana. The surname version was often spelled Spenser in the past, as in Edmund Spenser, the poet known for *The Faerie Queene*.

The protagonist of Henry James's short story *The Jolly Corner* is Spencer Brydon.

Stellan

Swedish, meaning unknown, possibly "calm"
Stellan is a strong, attractive, Scandinavian possible up-and-comer, known through actor Stellan Skarsgård, and his namesake, the son of Jennifer Connelly and Paul Bettany. Its

trendy "an" ending and the similarity in sound to the popular Kellen/Kellan make it all the more accessible.

Stone

Word name

Though some may find such names rather harsh and severe, increasing numbers of parents are gravitating toward this kind of flinty, steely, stony single-syllable name.

Many know the name via the distinguished TV newsman Stone Phillips; another bearer is Pearl Jam lead guitarist Stone Gossard. And yes, both were given the name at birth.

Sullivan

Irish surname, "black-eyed one"

Sullivan is a jaunty Celtic three-syllable name, with a real twinkle in its eye. It was immortalized in the 1930s classic film *Sullivan's Travels* and was chosen for one of Patrick Dempsey's twin boys. Nickname Sully is equally jaunty.

The third most common surname in Ireland, Sullivan's heritage dates back to the third century. Countless distinguished surnamed Sullivans include Sir Arthur, half of composing team Gilbert & Sullivan, Helen Keller's teacher Annie, Chicago architect Louis, early boxer John L. and dour columnist/TV emcee Ed.

Other celebs with boys named Sullivan: singer Tom Waits and actor James Marsters. Heroic pilot Chesley Sullenberger is known as Sully, and a featured character in Pixar's *Monsters, Inc.* is also Sulley.

Sven

Norse, "youth"

Especially for parents of Scandinavian descent, Sven is an accessible and attractive name with an appealing mix of strength and swagger. It comes from the ancient Swedish tribe, the Sviars, who gave their name to Svealand, which later morphed into Sweden.

Sven is now most popular not in its native Sweden but in The Netherlands, where it is currently in the Top 20.

An internationally noted bearer is Swedish cinematographer Sven Nykvist, known for his work on Ingmar Bergman films. Svens have appeared as characters in *Titanic*, Pixar's *Cars* (voiced by Arnold Schwarzenegger), as a Nintendo Pokémon and a manga character, and Marlon Brando portrayed an unlikely Sven in one of his late movies, *Free Money*.

Sweeney

Irish, "the little hero"

The double "e" gives this Celtic surname a genial sound. It derives from an old Irish name — Suibhne (SHEEV-ne) that was borne by several early saints and kings, including, unfortunately, one known as Mad Sweeney who spent his life living in trees and composing nature poetry. Another possible drawback is the association with Sweeney Todd, the bloodthirsty butcher of Sondheim stage-musical fame.

But if you can put all that aside, Sweeney makes a cheery choice.

Sylvester

Latin, "from the forest"

This name of three early popes has been associated in recent years with a cocky cartoon cat ("Thufferin' thuccatash!") and the Italian Stallion hero of the Rocky and Rambo movies (who was born Michael) — and yet we think it just might be ready to move further back into the mainstream.

Sylvester was at its height in the 1920s, when it was in the Top 200, and hung on in the lower rungs of the ladder until 1994. Lately, the name has been most visible as a surname — that of Sue Sylvester on *Glee*.

Trivia tidbit — in the 1935 movie Sylvia Scarlett, the young Katharine Hepburn disguises herself as a boy named Sylvester — until she meets Cary Grant!

T

Taj

Hindi, "crown"

Taj is a cool-sounding name reflecting the magnificence of the seventeenth-century Indian Taj Mahal, chosen by Aerosmith's Steven Tyler for his son.

The musician known as Taj Mahal was born Henry Saint Clair Fredericks. He claimed that his stage name came to him in dreams about India, Gandhi, and social tolerance.

Taj has actually made it onto the U.S. Top 1000 twice — in 1976 and 1998.

Tarquin

Roman clan name of uncertain meaning

One of the few ancient Roman names that don't end in "us," the rarely heard Tarquin has a decidedly creative, even dramatic flair, which could appeal to the parent looking for a strikingly original name. Sir Laurence Olivier used it for his oldest child, who was named Simon Tarquin but called by his middle name.

As Tarquinius, it was borne by two early kings of Rome.

Tarquin has some literary cred as well, appearing in Shakespeare's poem *The Rape of Lucrece* (referring to a dark stain on the name), as Tarquin Blackwood in Anne Rice's *The Vampire Chronicles* series and as Tarquin Cleath-Stuart in the *Shopaholic* series by Sophie Kinsella.

Tate

English from Norse, "cheerful"

A strong single-syllable surname with a joyful meaning, Tate is finding a place on more and more birth certificates. It's now at Number 391, having hovered in the Top 400 range for the past five years. Former Spice Girl Emma Bunton named her second son Tate Lee.

Tate also has a cultural vibe via the Tate and Tate Modern museums in London, named for philanthropist Henry Tate. Actor Tate Donovan is a prominent current bearer.

Tavish

Scottish variation of Thomas, "twin"
This Scottish form of Thomas has a lot of charm, evoking images of men in plaid kilts playing the bagpipes. As for the "ish" ending, it could either be seen as cozy and hamish, or a little wishy-washyish.

The Tavis version is associated these days with radio/TV personality Tavis Smiley.

Bottom line: If you're looking for a similar name with more ethnic appeal than Travis or an offbeat namesake for an ancestral Thomas, you could do well to consider Tavish.

Tennyson

English, "son of Dennis"
Few people would have considered the surname of this famous Victorian poet as a first name until Russell Crowe chose it for his son in 2006. But, as a rhythmic three-syllable patronymic, Tennyson has a lot going for it, not least of all the appealing nickname Tenny; it would make a novel choice for the son of a Dennis.

Other options: The poet's first name, Alfred, or the name of another esteemed bard, such as Eliot, Poe, Byron, Lowell or Lorca.

Thaddeus

Aramaic, meaning unclear, possibly from Theodore, "gift of God"
Thaddeus, a distinguished, long-neglected appellation, has several areas of appeal: a solid New Testament legacy, a nice antique feel, and the choice of several more modern nicknames and international variations — we particularly like the Italian Taddeo.

In the Bible, Thaddeus was one of the original Twelve Apostles, who is referred to variously as Lebbaeus, whose surname was Thaddaeus, as Judas the son of James, and as Judas, not Iscariot — many believing that Thaddeus was the surname used to distinguish him from the treacherous Judas Iscariot.

Thaddeus has made any number of screen appearances in vehicles ranging from *Spongebob Squarepants* to *Police Academy* to *Get Smart* (it was the given name of the Chief) to *Harry Potter*. As Tadzio — the Slavic version — he played a leading role in Thomas Mann's *Death in Venice*.

In real life, Taddeo Gaddi was a renowned Renaissance painter and Thaddeus Stevens was a dominant political figure during the Civil War, played by Tommy Lee Jones in *Lincoln*.

Thatcher

English occupational name, "roof thatcher"

Thatcher is an open and friendly freckle-faced surname, fresher sounding than Tyler or Taylor, that dates back to the days of thatched-roof cottages.

Britberries in particular may have strong associations to Prime Minister Margaret, but the surname has other notable bearers as well, such as Becky Thatcher, the object of Tom's affections in *The Adventures of Tom Sawyer*. Thatcher Grey is the protagonist's father on *Grey's Anatomy*, and TV celebrity chef Cat Cora has a son named Thatcher Julius.

Thelonious

Latinized variation of German Tillman, "one who plows the earth"
One of the coolest of names, thanks to legendary jazz pianist Thelonious Sphere Monk, who inherited this Latin-sounding German name from his father. It has been used very sparingly since the 1960s, with just a sprinkling of baby boys receiving the name each year.

Monk's middle name Sphere is pretty unique too — a cousin of Cosmos and Cosmo.

Theo

Diminutive of Theodore, "gift of God"

Many modern parents use Theo as the short form for Theodore rather than the dated Ted — including some celebs, such as Dallas Bryce Howard — but others bypass the Grandpa name Theodore entirely and skip right to the hip nickname Theo. Short and ultra-chic, Theo's a cool, contemporary baby name choice.

Theo first made an impact as the name of the only son on *The Cosby Show*; earlier, it was associated with Vincent Van Gogh's supportive brother Theo.

Theo is currently having a burst of popularity in Europe, ranking in the Top 20 in Sweden, France and Belgium — and 2011 was the second year Theo made it into the U.S. Top 1000. Now it's at Number 794, up over 60 points this year alone with every indication of moving higher.

Theodore

Greek, "gift of God"
When Theodore Roosevelt took office in 1901, the name Theodore was in the Top 40, with Teds and Teddys everywhere. After some damaging stereotypes — the chubby Chipmunk Theodore, and Beaver Cleaver's real name — Theodore went into a decline, from which it has definitely made a recovery, thanks in part to the popular nickname Theo.

Theodore has been the choice of several celebrities, including Bryce Dallas Howard, Natascha McElhone and Ali Larter.

The name has a distinguished history; in addition to being presidential, it was borne by novelist Dreiser, poet Roethke, French painter Gericault, and was the first name of Dr. Seuss.

Among the well-known Teds, baseball's Williams and musician Nugent were born Theodore, but Ted Turner was christened Robert, and Ted Kennedy and Ted Danson were originally Edward.

The beloved character Laurie in *Little Women* was named Theodore Laurence.

Thomas

Aramaic, "twin"
Thomas has been one of the most commonly used classic baby names in both England and the U.S., and is still given to almost seven thousand American boys each year. From the original apostle and several saints, through Thomas Jefferson, Edison, Hanks and Cruise, Thomas is simple, straightforward and strong — all that a parent with timeless taste could want. And as a bonus, kids will identify with *Thomas the Tank Engine*.

Thomas came about because there were too many apostles named Judas; Jesus renamed one Thomas (meaning "twin") to distinguish him from Judas Iscariot and the Judas also known as Thaddeus, and at first it was used only for priests. Sir Thomas Aquinas and Thomas à Becket are two of many towering Thomases.

Thomas ranked among the U.S. Top 10 baby names pretty much through the 1960s; right now it is still Number 6 in Britain and Number 7 in Australia.

Thomas has some noteworthy foreign versions: the multicultural Tomas, the Italian Tomasso, the Portuguese Tomaz, plus the Scottish nickname Tam. In Paris these days, Tom is a popular name used on its own,

Jack Black and Dennis Quaid both have sons named Thomas.

Thor

Norse, "thunder"
Thor is the powerful name of the Norse god of thunder, strength, and rain would make a bold statement. Long a comic book staple, Thor has now invaded the big screen, and could land on birth certificates as well.

Thor Heyerdahl was a famous Norwegian anthropologist/adventurer, author of the book *Kon Tiki*.

In Norse mythology, Thor was the son of Odin — another crossover name possibility — who was sometimes referred to as Bjorn in Old Norse poetry. Tor is a popular variation (which is also the Hebrew name of a bird that symbolizes the arrival of spring).

Tiberius

Latin, "of the Tiber"

The name of an important ancient Roman emperor, Tiberius might sound a bit heavy for a modern boy to carry, but with the rise of Atticus, Tiberius and brothers begin to feel more baby-friendly, much in the same way as Old Testament names like Elijah and Isaiah have been rejuvenated.

The contemporary ear has become attuned to the name via some modern sagas. There were two Tiberiuses in the *Harry Potter* universe: T. McLaggen, uncle of Cormac, and T. Ogden, a former member of the Wizengamot. Peter O'Toole played Emperor Tiberius Caesar in the 1979 *Caligula*, and James Tiberius Kirk was Captain of the USS Enterprise on *Star Trek*.

Tiernan

Irish, "lord, chief"

Tiernan is the slightly edgier and more seductive cousin of Kiernan. This is one Irish surname that is attractive but distinctive; Tierney is another, related, option.

Tiernan was a popular name in early and medieval Ireland and was borne by several kings and saints. It is currently high on the list in Northern Ireland.

Tierney

Irish, "descendant of a lord"

Tierney is a Celtic surname with a definite Irish twinkle, a name just waiting to be discovered. Though now sometimes used for girls (in the U.S., not Ireland), as in jazz singer Tierney Sutton, it still has plenty of masculine punch.

Tierney, in its original Tiarnach form, was the name of several saints. It can also join the ranks of Old Hollywood names, via the haunting actress Gene Tierney. *ER* actress Maura Tierney is a current surname bearer.

Titus

Latin, meaning unknown

Titus, once seen as a slightly forbidding Roman, New Testament, and Shakespearean name, was brought back to contemporary life by the TV series *Titus 2000*, and is now, at Number 360, by far the highest it's ever ranked, increasing in popularity along with other revived ancient names like Linus and Silas.

In the New Testament, Titus was a trusted companion of St. Paul, the recipient of one of his epistles; from Shakespeare the name is familiar via the central character of his tragedy *Titus Andronicus*, as well as appearing in *Antony and Cleopatra*, *Coriolanus* and *Timon of Athens*. Titus Groan is the protagonist of Mervyn Peake's *Gormenghast Gothic* fantasy trilogy, and Titus Welliver was a character on *Deadwood*.

The painter Rembrandt had a son named Titus.

Tobias

Greek from Hebrew, "God is good"
Tobias is one of a number of "s" ending boys' names that are riding a wave of popularity, now at the midpoint of the Social Security list and poised to rise.

With its Old Testament-Dickensian feel, it's a name with a distinguished pedigree — Tobias Smollett, for instance, was a major eighteenth-century Scottish novelist — that also has a contemporary feel. A contemporary bearer is Tobias Wolff, author of *A Boy's Life*; Tobias Snape is a *Harry Potter* character.

Tobias is the name of several biblical figures, but is primarily associated with the story of Tobias and the Angel.

Tobias is currently popular in Europe: it's the second most popular name in Austria and Number 11 in Norway.

The short form Toby has a life of its own, used independently at least as far back as Shakespeare's time, with Sir Toby Belch in *Twelfth Night*. Toby was the name of a character on *The West Wing*, and is currently at Number 54 in England. Actor Tobey Maguire was born Tobias and named his son Otis Tobias.

There is also the rarely used but still viable daddy of them all, Tobiah, the name of a rebel Hebrew king.

Tolliver

English occupational name, "metalworker"
If you're tired of Oliver, you might consider this energetic three-syllable surname instead, so you could have a little Tolly instead of an Ollie.

Tolliver is a not-too-obvious occupational Scottish surname dating back to the time of armor makers. Heard much more often as a surname, there have been Tollivers in soap operas like *General Hospital* and Cy Tolliver was a character on *Deadwood*; in real life, Melba Tolliver is a barrier-breaking African-American TV journalist.

Torquil

Scottish from Norse, "Thor's cauldron"

Torquil, is a quirky but intriguing option that evolved from an ancient Scandinavian name and was imported into Scotland by the Vikings. The Gaelic form of the name is Torcaill.

Torquil MacLeod was the name of an early Scottish clan chief.

Trent

English, "the flooder"

This strong single-syllable boy's name has been finding favor with parents since the 50s, and is still at Number 380. Its main associations have been with the River Trent, whose name dates back to prehistoric times, and with long-serving Mississippi Senator Trent (born Chester) Lott, and Trent Reznor (born Michael) of Nine Inch Nails.

In the eighteenth century, William Trent founded a settlement, which became the city known as Trenton (Trent's town), and that morphed into a first name for boys, which now ranks at Number 239.

(James) Trent Olson is the only brother of the three Olson sisters; Trent Ford has been seen on *Gosford Park*, *The West Wing* and *Vampire Diaries*. And the name of the Vince Vaughn character in the 1996 movie *Swingers* is Trent.

Tristan

Celtic, meaning unknown

Tristan — known through medieval legend and Wagnerian opera — has a slightly wistful, touching air. This, combined with the name's popular "an" ending, makes Tristan very appealing to parents seeking a more original alternative to Christian.

Tristan has been growing in popularity since the 1970s, moving in and out of the Top 100 since 1996, now at Number 89. One influence was the character Tristan Ludlow played by Brad Pitt in the 1994 movie *Legends of the Fall*, based on a Jim Harrison novel.

Tristan is a dragon-slaying hero of Celtic legend, whose story was incorporated into Malory's *Le Morte d'Arthur*, in which Tristan is one of the Knights of the Round Table, consumed by his doomed love affair with Queen Isolde. Wagner set the story to music in his opera *Tristan und Isolde*.

Tristan and its alternate form Tristram have been found in later lit as well. *Tristram Shandy* is a famous early comic novel by Laurence Sterne (in which the hero's father calls Tristram the worst name in the universe); Tristan is a major character in James Herriott's *All Creatures Great and Small*, and there is an eponymous novella by Thomas Mann.

Particularly popular in Canada, Tristan was chosen for their sons by Travis Tritt, Wayne Gretzky and Natasha Henstridge.

Other variants of Tristan include Tristen, Tristin, Triston and Tristian.

Truman
English, "loyal one"

Truman, an upstanding presidential name that radiates an aura of integrity and moral truth, values any parent would want for her child, seems definitely headed for a revival.

Also associated with writer Truman Capote, Truman was at its height of popularity in the early years of the twentieth century, around the time Capote was born. It reached its highest point — Number 248 — in 1945, the year Harry Truman succeeded FDR.

Tom Hanks and Rita Wilson chose it for their son, and it's also the name of Martha Stewart's young grandson.

Truman Burbank was the ingenuous character played by Jim Carrey in *The Truman Show*" and Truman was the surname of Will in *Will and Grace*.

Tucker
English occupational name, "fabric pleater"

Tucker has more spunk than most last-name-first-names, and also a positive, comforting ("Tuck me in, Mommy") feel.

Tucker got something of a preppy image via bow-tied conservative TV commentator Tucker Carlson, and quite the opposite from writer/blogger Tucker Max, author of the Number 1 best-seller *I Hope They Serve Beer in Hell*. Tucker Crowe is a character in the Nick Hornby novel *Juliet, Naked*.

Tully
Irish, "flood, peaceful, or hill"

Tully is a relaxed, rarely used Irish surname possibility. Sources disagree on the meaning, depending on what root is used. The Irish *tulach* means hill or mound, while *tuile* means flood. Other sources relate it to the Roman Tullius, most notably the name of the philosopher Marcus Tullius Cicero, sometimes anglicized as Tully. Statesman Alexander Hamilton used the pen name Tully when he wrote editorials denouncing the instigators of the Whiskey Rebellion.

The ancient Irish name Tuathal, which is translated as Tully, was given to many Irish kings and heroes.

Turner

English occupational name, "works with a lathe"

Turner is a name that's both preppy and painterly, recalling the exquisite watercolor seascapes of British painter J. M. W. An occupational name in the Taylor-Carter mold, Turner is a more distinctive choice than many of the usual suspects.

One first-name Turner namesake is Turner Catledge, the first Executive Editor of the New York Times, but for the most part its more notable bearers were surnamed Turner: Nat, the leader of a slave rebellion and subject of a William Styron novel, media mogul Ted, musicians Ike and Tina, and glamour girl Lana. In the movie *Turner & Hooch*, Tom Hanks was Det. Scott Turner and Hooch was the dog.

U

Ulysses

Latin variation of the Greek Odysseus

Ulysses is one of the few "U" boys' names anyone knows — with heavy links to the Homeric hero, eighteenth president Grant (christened Hiram Ulysses), and the James Joyce novel — all of which makes it both distinguished and kind of weighty for a modern boy.

Former *SNL*er Anna Gasteyer made this bold choice for her son, perhaps inspiring others to follow her lead. George Clooney's character name in the Coen brothers' *O Brother, Where Art Thou?* is Ulysses.

Trivia tidbit: The presidential bearer was christened Hiram Ulysses Grant, but reputedly was all too happy when his first two names were inadvertently reversed at West Point, as he had always been embarrassed by having the initials HUG.

Urban

Latin, "of the city"

Urban was not an uncommon name through the 1930s (rising as high as Number 435), having been attached to several saints and early popes, but it has completely disappeared from the landscape — both urban and rural. Yet in this era of word name appreciation and trend for "an"-ending boys' names, we're thinking it might be ready for a return.

In the New Testament, Urban is an active member of the Christian church in Rome.

Urbano is the commonly heard Italian version, and the French Urbain was used by Henry James for a — yes — urbane character in *The American*.

These days, the name is associated with musician Keith Urban.

Uri

Hebrew, "my flame, my light"

This short but strong name, commonly heard in Israel, has a lot of crossover potential, and is among the most usable on the minuscule menu of "U" names.

The are two Uris in the Old Testament — the father of Bezalel, an artisan blessed with the skill to create the meeting tent and ark of the covenant for Moses, and the father of Geber, one of the twelve officials who provided nourishment for Solomon. Uri is a symbolic name for boys born on Hanukkah.

Notable bearers: Uri Geller, self-proclaimed paranormalist known for his spoon bending on *The Tonight Show*; and prize-winning children's book writer and illustrator Uri Shulevitz.

Longer related names: Uriah, the archangel, and Uriel.

V

Valentine

Latin, "healthy, strong"

Valentine is an attractive Shakespearean name with romantic associations, but those very ties to the saint and the sentimental holiday have sent it into a decline, one which we think may be about to turn around.

The name's best known bearer is the third-century martyr St. Valentine, whose feast day of February 14th coincided with the pagan fertility festival of the goddess Juno, all of which led to the modern Valentine's Day.

There are two Shakespearean characters named Valentine: one in *Twelfth Night*, and the other belonging to one of the two gentlemen in *Two Gentlemen of Verona*.

Victor

Latin, "conqueror"

Victor made it big in the English-speaking world during the reign of Queen Victoria, one of the few male names popularized by a female version.

Victor was the first name of Dr. Frankenstein, the scholar who brings the monster to life, and the romantic figure of Victor Laszlo in Casablanca, not to mention the esteemed writer Victor Hugo.

Victor is currently popular in Denmark (where it's Number 5), Belgium (14) and Spain (32). Italian version Vittorio adds a large measure of charm.

Viggo

Scandinavian, "war"

Though to most Americans Viggo is a one-person name attached to intense actor Mortensen, it is actually an old Norse name dating back to the Vikings, and is currently the 32nd most popular appellation in Sweden. Viggo Mortensen is a Jr, sharing his name with his Danish father. We think this name is so, well, vigorous, that it might appeal to others as well. Taylor and Natalie Hanson seemed to agree when they chose it for their fourth child.

Vincent

Latin, "conquering"

Vincent is a name with a complex image; after being quietly used for centuries, it is suddenly seeming stylish, along with other "V" names. Even the nickname Vince has been given a reprieve via actor Vince Vaughn and country singer Vince Gill.

Vincent was popular during the Middle Ages, especially among the French, who brought it to England. There are a number of St. Vincents, most famous of whom is St. Vincent de Paul, a seventeenth-century French priest who organized societies of laymen to help the poor.

Vincent has always been a favorite of Roman Catholic families, particularly in the Italian community. Its most notable bearer was Vincent Van Gogh, but there have also been philanthropist Vincent Astor, who gave it a patrician edge, and actors Vincent Price and Vincent D'Onofrio.

Vincent/Vince/Vinny has appeared recently on screen as the central characters of *My Cousin Vinny* and *Entourage."* John Travolta had two key Vin-roles, as Vinnie Barbarino in the TV series that launched him, *Welcome Back, Kotter,* and as Vincent Vega in *Pulp Fiction.* Vincent was the gentle giant on TV's *Beauty and the Beast,* and Ethan Hawke played a Vincent in *Gattaca.*

Virgil

Latin, "staff bearer"

The name of the greatest Roman poet and an early Irish saint who believed the earth was round, Virgil is rarely heard nowadays, but it retains a certain pleasantly fusty feel and likable southern twang. The first-century poet known as Virgil, author of the influential epic *Aeneid,* was christened Publius Vergilius Maro. Centuries later, Virgil Tibbs was the noble police detective portrayed by Sidney Poitier in two films, *In the Heat of the Night* and *They Call Me Mr. Tibbs.* Currently, Virgil Minelli is a character on *The Mentalist.*

Virgil was the name of one of Wyatt Earp's brothers, a Tombstone, Arizona Marshall, Virgil Thomson was a noted composer and musicologist, cartoonist Virgil Franklin Partch signed his work VIP, and astronaut Gus Grissom was born Virgil.

Virgil's greatest popularity took place in the early decades of the twentieth century: It was a Top 100 name for five years.

Vladimir

Slavic, "renowned prince"

Vladimir, which has a musical prodigy kind of vibe, is a cultured Russian name associated in this country with piano virtuoso Vladimir Horowitz and the author of *Lolita,* Vladimir Nabokov.

Vladimir is rich in history as well, being the name of the first Christian ruler of Russia, who became the patron saint of that country's Catholic church; Lenin, the founder of the USSR, and current President Putin.

A common name throughout Russia, Vladimir is featured in novels by Turgenev and Pushkin. Vladimir also has vampirish connections: Dracula is based on Vlad III, otherwise known as — oops — Vlad the Impaler. A more modern literary character is Vladimir, one of the two main figures in Samuel Beckett's play *Waiting for Godot*.

W

Walden

English, "valley of the Welsh"

Walden is a recent entrant to the "en" ending boys' names trend, a name that summons up placid images of Thoreau's two-year stay contemplating nature near Walden Pond.

A quite different image came into being when Walden was chosen as the name for Ashton Kutcher's character in *Two and a Half Men* — internet billionaire Walden Schmidt. It is also a *Harry Potter* name, via wizard Walden Macnair.

Waldo

German, pet form of names such as Waldemar, "to rule"

Its jaunty "o" ending makes this name more appealing than most of its Germanic brothers, and we hope we're beyond the constant response to his name being "Where's Waldo?" The weighty reputation of writer and philosopher Ralph Waldo Emerson adds a measure of backbone to the name.

In tribute to Ralph Waldo, many babies were given those two names, including Ralph (Waldo) Ellison, author of *Invisible Man*.

In popular culture, the young Robert Redford played the dashing titular character in *The Great Waldo Pepper*, and Waldo Lydecker was a key character in the haunting classic film *Laura*.

Walker

English occupational name, "cloth-walker"

Walker is both a WASP-y surname name — as in the *W* in George W. Bush — but it also has a gentle ambling quality and a creative connection to such greats as writer Walker Percy and photographer Walker Evans, whose father was also named Walker.

As a common surname, Walker has many other notable namesakes, including author Alice, football great Herschel Walker, blues guitarist T-Bone, and contemporary artist Kara.

Walker was a popular first name around the turn of the last century, reaching Number 296 in 1896, remained in use through 1955, then made a return in 1983, becoming a prime representative of the aspirational surnames of the 1980s and 90s. It's now at Number 411.

Walter

German, "army ruler"

Walter was seen as a noble name in the Sir Walter Raleigh and Sir Walter Scott era, but has long been in baby name limbo. Now a few independent-minded parents are looking at it as a renewable, slightly quirky, classic, stronger and more distinctive than James or John.

A favorite Norman name, Walter was extremely popular in medieval England (when it was pronounced "Water"), and in this country from the 1870s through the 1940s. Plus there are all those great Walters and Walts to consider, from Whitman to Disney to Cronkite to Mondale to Payton to Matthau to the ultimate fantasizer Walter Mitty, not to mention (Walter) Bruce Willis.

Actor Rainn Wilson named his son Walter.

Watson

English and Scottish, "son of Wat," a pet form of Walter, "army ruler"

What with the resurgence of "W" names like Weston and Walter, the prominence of high profile actress Emma and golfer Bubba, and even the attention paid to Watson, the IBM computer on *Jeopardy* (named for IBM's founder, Thomas Watson) this name could be in line for a revival of its own.

Watson is the twentieth most common surname in Scotland, and among the earliest emigrants to the Virginia Colony from England was John Watson in 1635. Later noted bearers of the surname include Alexander Graham Bell's telephone experiment partner Thomas A. Watson ("Mr. Watson — come here!"), James Watson, co-discoverer of DNA, and actress Emily. Two well-known Watsons in fiction are Sherlock Holmes's accomplice, Dr (John) Watson, and Spider-Man's love interest, Mary Jane. All in all: a name with a varied and fascinating heritage.

Waylon

English, "land beside the road"

Country singer Waylon Jennings bestowed a kind of outlaw image on his name. In the past two years, Waylon has jumped about 100 places in terms of popularity, climbing along with other cowboyish names.

Waylon Jennings's son, also named Waylon, is called Shooter, and Shooter's young son, Waylon Albert, (with actress wife Drea DeMatteo) will be addressed as Blackjack.

Grandpa Jennings was originally called Wayland, but the name was changed early on by his mother.

Webb

English occupational name, "weaver"

This pleasant single-syllable surname might be especially appealing to someone involved with the internet (and who isn't?) — even if some others might see it as a drawback.

Webb is one of those names that were well used at the end of the nineteenth century — it was Number 567 in 1880 — and then completely vanished. One possible namesake is the honky tonk singer Webb Pierce.

Webb is much more visible as a surname, some notable bearers being actors Jack, Clifton, Chloe and Veronica, jazz musician Chick, and British reformer Beatrice.

Webster

English occupational name, "weaver"

Webster is one of several "W" starting surname names back on the drawing board, now that it has recovered from its childlike 80s sitcom identity.

Webster was used in respectable numbers in the past — it reached a high of Number 388 in 1890 — but like several other surnames starting with "W," fell off the list completely in the 1940s. With its engaging nickname Webb, we can see it making a comeback.

Webster Young was a jazz trumpeter who played with most of the greats, but more prominent bearers wore Webster as a surname — in particular statesman Daniel and lexicographer Noah.

Wesley

English, "western meadow"

Wesley is one of a group of "W" starting surname names reminiscent of the Old West that are making a comeback, now in the Top 160 — though not as well used as it was in the 1970s, when he ranked as high as Number 66.

Many boys given this English place name in the past were done so to honor the founder of Methodism, John Wesley, and his influential brother Charles, who probably came from one of the various towns in England called Westley. The use of the appellation as a first name began during their lifetime, but its use has spread independent of its religious associations.

Two well-known bearers of the name are retired general and one-time presidential hopeful Wesley Clark and actor Wesley Snipes. A pair of movie directors known by their nicknames, Wes Anderson and Wes Craven, were born as Wesley, while jazz guitarist

Wes Montgomery was christened John Leslie. Many people will associate the name with John Wesley Hardin, celebrated by both Johnny Cash and Bob Dylan in song.

Wesley Crusher is a character from *Star Trek: The Next Generation*, and Wesley Wyndam-Pryce appeared *in Buffy the Vampire Slayer* and, more prominently, in *Angel*.

West

Word name

West is the most fashionable of what you might call the direction names, with North and East (or Easton and Easter) coming up behind, and South not yet on the map.

Country singer Randy Houser named his baby boy West Yantz, but West is definitely shaping up to be a unisex name: West Flynn is the daughter of Marley Shelton, Teá Leoni and David Ducovney named their girl Madelaine West, and Maura West put her surname into middle place for her daughter Birdie.

Weston

English, "from the western town"

Weston has gone from being a Jane Austenish British surname to a first name with a relaxed American western cowboy feel. Along with other trendy "n" ending boys' names, Weston is rising in popularity, moving from Number 203 to 171 — its highest ever — last year. Weston also has a glimmer of creative appeal via its connection to the great photographer Edward Weston. Nicolas Cage chose Weston for his son back in 1990, when it was much more unusual; *The Office*'s Jenna Fischer used it for her baby more recently. Cousin name Easton is even more popular, currently at Number 96.

Wheeler

English occupational name, "wheel maker"

Wheeler is one of the most energetic of the newly stylish occupational names, all those "e"s giving it a friendly, freewheeling sound.

Wheeler has some historical cred via the nineteenth Vice President of the United States, William Almon Wheeler.

Wilder

Surname or word name

Though it hasn't yet appeared in the Top 1000, Wilder is on many parents' possibility lists, one of the new generation of bad boy names growing in popularity. Wilder got a big boost in interest through Goldie Hawn's grandson via son Oliver, born in 2007.

Wilder is more familiar as a surname, borne by such notables as authors Laura Ingalls and Thornton, composer Alec, director Billy, actor Gene, and Douglas Wilder, the first African-American to be elected Governor of Virginia.

Will

Diminutive of William, "resolute protection"
Will has definitely replaced Bill, not only as a nickname for William but as a stand-alone name as well, partly thanks to England's Prince William, also known as Wills.

Will has a nice old-fashioned, down-home charm, and with recent references such as Will Smith, *Good Will Hunting* and *Will and Grace*, it has taken on an air of understated cool.

Most celebrities known as Will were christened William — Shakespeare, of course, legendary humorist Rogers, cartoonist Eisner and actor Arnett — but others were not. Will Smith was born Willard and Will Ferrell was originally John William.

A key character on *Glee* is Will Schuester.

William

English from German, "resolute protection"
William has been among the most enduring of classics, currently standing at a solid Number 5. In the last year, the name has been chosen by almost 17,000 American parents as being ideally conservative yet contemporary. For 400 years, William has been second only to John as the most popular name in the English-speaking world. And now of course it's also a newsy name, thanks to Britain's high-profile Prince William.

In terms of short forms, yesterday's Bills and Billys have given way to today's Wills — or Williams, with no diminutive — though a few hip Billys, including Helena Bonham Carter and Tim Burton's, have surfaced recently. But Will, sometimes used on its own, is still the most stylish William nickname.

The name was introduced to England by William the Conqueror, and has long reigned as a royal name in the U.K. There are tons of worthy namesakes called William, including Williams Shakespeare, Blake, Saroyan and Faulkner, Will Rogers, Bill Gates, and four U.S. presidents.

Willoughby

English, "farm near the willows"
Willoughby is an energetic last-name-first route to the popular short form Will, livelier than any of the two-syllable options. It could be picked up by parents attracted to the Willow sound for girls.

Willoughby Patterne is the protagonist of the George Meredith novel, *The Egotist*. Willoughby Sharp was a contemporary artist, curator, critic, and founder of the seminal art magazine, *Avalanche*. There is a classic 1962 British children's novel titled *The Wolves of Willoughby Chase* by Joan Aiken that was made into a film in 1989.

Wilson

English, "son of Will"

Wilson is a substantive presidential choice far less prevalent than Taylor or Tyler, and with the advantage of being a new route to friendly nickname Will. We see Wilson growing in popularity as an alternative to William; and as a patronymic, it would make a conceivable (if possibly confusing) choice for a son of William.

Being the tenth most common surname in the U.S., Wilson has countless possible last-named namesakes in every field, from politics to show biz. Those with Wilson as a first name are harder to find, beyond soul singer-songwriter Wilson Pickett and Wilson Rawls, author of the beloved book *Where the Red Fern Grows*. Wilson is also the name of Tom Hank's friend, the volleyball, in the movie *Castaway*.

Winston

English, "wine's town"

Long associated with the Churchill family and common in the West Indies, the distinguished Winston has tended to be neglected here. The exception was during the World War II period, when Winston Churchill was a towering figure and his name reached Number 234.

Winston Smith is the main character in George Orwell's *1984*, is a presence in *Pulp Fiction*, is the name of a character in the best-selling book and film *How Stella Got Her Groove Back*, and was John Lennon's middle name. Billie Piper and Laurence Fox named their son Winston in 2008.

With the current trend towards using hero names, we can see this upstanding Anglo-Saxon example making a return.

The nickname Winnie came into the public consciousness with the *Winnie-the-Pooh* books, but is now almost exclusively feminine — though you can shorten it further to the winning Win.

Minor irritant: Connection to the cigarette brand.

Wolf

German, "wolf"; diminutive of Wolfgang, "traveling wolf"

Wolf is a name with a split personality. It can be seen as one of the fierce animal names, like Fox and Bear and Puma, with a touch of the werewolf, or it can be viewed as a quieter, Wolf Blitzer kind of name, fairly common in German (where is pronounced Vulf) and Jewish families, sometimes as a short form of Wolfgang.

CNN newscaster Blitzer inherited the name from his grandfather. Other Wolfs of note include British screenwriter Wolf Mankowitz, who was instrumental in the early James Bond films, painter Wolf Kahn, and the hero of Jack London's 1904 novel *The Sea-Wolf*, Wolf Larsen.

Nickname Wolfie definitely domesticates it.

Wyatt

English surname, "brave in war"

Wyatt has been hot, which is to say cool, for several years now. With its easy Wyatt Earp-ish cowboy charm, it's relaxed but still highly respectable.

Wyatt got one of its first modern pushes when Peter Fonda played a Wyatt in the seminal film *Easy Rider*. Now, at Number 41, it is the highest it has ever been in this country. Goldie Hawn and Kurt Russell were among the first celebs to use Wyatt for their son born in 1986; more recently, singer Sheryl Crow chose it for her baby boy.

Wyatt is also enjoying a wave of current popularity in Canada.

Wylie

English, "from Wylye"

Wylie is a friendly, nonchalant rodeo name with an almost irresistible charm; parents may pick up on its pleasant similarity to the more popular, unisex Riley. Although more masculine, we see Wylie as working as well for boys and girls (Richard Anderson used it for his daughter in 1999). Wylie (or the interchangeable Wiley) can also be an original and authentic way to honor an ancestral William. We don't, however, recommend you spell the name the way Corey Parker did: Wylei. Why lay?

Wiley Post was the first to solo pilot a plane around the world, and contemporary foodies know Wylie Dufresne as a renowned chef, a leading proponent of the molecular gastronomy movement. Elinor Wylie was an inspirational poet.

X

Xander

Diminutive of Alexander, Greek, "defending men"

One of the newer short forms of Alexander, Xander is a spelling that first saw the spotlight via *Buffy the Vampire Slayer*, and then as Vin Diesel's character in *XXX*. This relative newcomer, along with phonetic spelling Zander, is now in the Top 300 names in the country. *Mad Men* star January Jones named her son Xander Dane.

Even shorter forms Xan and Zan are now also being used on their own. Xan is a character in the P. D. James novel *The Children of Men*, and is a favorite choice of computer game creators.

Xavier

Basque, "new house"; Arabic, "bright"

Xavier is one of the only "x" names most people know and use, often as a middle name following Francis, as in Saint Francis Xavier, cofounder of the Jesuit order, who got his name from the Spanish-Basque village where he was born.

Today's parents are beginning to reassess Xavier, now just outside the Top 80 — almost the highest it's ever been ranked. It is popular in several countries, and is in the Top 15 in Quebec.

Xavier was chosen for their sons by Donnie Wahlberg and Tilda Swinton — as well as the middle name of Larenz Tate's son Miles. Note that though that initial "x" does have a distinct appeal, the correct pronunciation has it beginning with a "z" sound.

The Spanish classic Javier, pronounced HAH-vee-ay, has come into greater prominence via Oscar-winning Javier Bardem.

Trivia note: the X-men comics introduced the kree8iv spelling Xzavier.

Z

Zachariah

Hebrew, form of Zechariah, "the Lord has remembered"
This distinguished name still feels a bit ancient, but with the rise of such former graybeards as Jeremiah and Elijah, it also sounds child-friendly again, as does the Latin-Greek form Zacharias.

Zachariah is a name that was in fairly regular use by the Puritans of the sixteenth century, then was eventually and completely overtaken by the more modern sounding Zachary. But strange as it may seem, Zachariah and Zacharias now seem more au courant than Zachary.

In the Bible, spelled Zechariah, it is the name of about thirty different personages, one of whom gave his name to the book of Zechariah.

Zarachiah Hobson is a character in the Thackaray novel, *The Newcomes*.

Zakkai, a Hebrew abbreviation of Zachariah, is another interesting option.

Zan

Diminutive of Alexander, Greek, "defending men"
There's Zan and there's Xan — take your pick. Both of these are the latest generation of Alexander nicknames, Xan having been noticed first as a character on *Buffy the Vampire Slayer* (a rich source of names), and soon phoneticized into Zan. The spellings are running neck and neck in popularity, with Xan slightly ahead, while other parents prefer the longer forms, Xander and Zander, both of which also rank in the two hundreds.

Zane

Possible variation of John, "God is gracious"
Western novelist Zane (born Pearl!) Grey made this name famous. Now, it's in tune with the style of our times, retaining that appealing cowboy image.

Zane Grey was the great-grandson of Ebenezer Zane, founder of Zanesville, Ohio, the town where the writer was born. The name Zane has been on the popularity list since 1921, the heyday of such Zane Grey novels as *The Riders of the Purple Sage*.

Some parents — including country singer Mindy McCready, have begun to use the spelling Zayne.

Zebadiah

Hebrew, "God has bestowed"

Biblical names are expanding (literally) as some parents move on from Isaiah and Elijah to more elaborate choices like Jedidiah or Zebadiah with simple short forms like Jed and Zeb.

If you like this style of name, there are also a number of others to choose from — Zedekiah (the last king of Judah), Zecheriah (there are 31 in the Bible), Zachariah, the prophet Zephaniah, and Jedidiah, the name given to Solomon at his birth.

Zebedee

English variation of Hebrew Zebadiah, "God has bestowed"

Zebedee is an adorable and unusual New Testament name — which may sound like but is not a contradiction in terms. Unlike some of the longer biblical Z-names, Zebedee has a more lighthearted usability, with its gleeful "ee" ending. And Zeb makes a fabulous nickname.

In the New Testament, Zebedee plays the major role of the fisherman father of two disciples, James and John, and was with his sons mending his fishing nets when they were called by Christ.

The name was popularized in the U.K. by a jack-in-the-box puppet named Zebedee on an early kids' TV show, *The Magic Roundabout*.

Zebedee Jones is a contemporary British painter.

Zebulon

Hebrew, "exaltation or little dwelling"

An Old Testament name with a Puritan feel and post-Zachary possibilities — one of several routes to the cool nickname Zeb.

Pike's Peak was named for Zebulon Pike, the best-known bearer of the name.

In the Bible, Zebulon — or Zebulun — was the son of Jacob and Leah, the ancestor of the tribe of Israel which bore his name and settled around Nazareth. The Zebulunites mustered the single largest army to fight for David's installation as king.

Zeno

Anglicized form of Greek Zenon, related to Zeus, king of the gods

Zeno, the name of two ancient philosophers, has a muscular dynamism that's lightened by its cheerful final vowel, resulting in a kind of offbeat sci-fi feel. Zeno of Citium was the founder of the Stoic school of thought, Zeno of Elea was another early, original Greek thinker, famed for his Paradoxes.

Zeno Cosini is the protagonist of the Italo Svevo novel *Confessions of Zeno*.

Zephyr

Greek, "west wind"

If you're looking for a boy's name that's light and breezy, this could be it. A name from mythology: Zephyrus/Zephyr was the Greek god of the west wind — with many European variations, it's a name that's frequently seen in computer and video games, is a character in the children's book *Silverwing*, and appears in the *Babar* books — as a monkey.

Robby Benson and Karla DeVito named their son Zephyr in 1992, and Zephyr Benson is now a fledgling actor himself.

Zion

Hebrew, "highest point"

Zion has taken off in recent years, especially after singer Lauryn Hill used it for her son in 1997. It combines a user-friendly Ryan-Brian sound with the gravitas of religious significance. The Hebrew pronunciation is "tziyon."

In the Old Testament, the name Zion frequently refers to the city of Jerusalem as a whole, and came to be symbolic of Jewish national aspirations, and thus was the source of the term Zionism.

Basketball star Dwayne Wade and model Isabel Fontana also named their sons Zion, and reality star Fantasia Barrino bestowed it on her daughter.

Zion now stands at Number 235 for boys — representing about 1,500 baby Zions born in 2012 — and at Number 778 for girls.

THE LIST

Aaron	Archer	Baxter	Bruno
Abbott	Archibald	Baz	Burl
Abel	Archie	Beau	Byron
Abelard	Ari	Becan	Cade
Abijah	Arjun	Beckett	Cagney
Abner	Arlo	Benedict	Caleb
Abraham	Arrow	Benjamin	Calixto
Abraxas	Arthur	Bennett	Calloway
Absalom	Asa	Benno	Callum
Ace	Asher	Bing	Calvin
Adair	Atticus	Birch	Canyon
Adlai	Auberon	Bix	Carson
Alaric	Auden	Bjorn	Carter
Alcott	August	Blaise	Carver
Alec	Augustine	Boaz	Casper
Alessandro	Augustus	Bodhi	Caspian
Alexander	Aurelius	Booker	Cassian
Alfie	Autry	Boris	Cassius
Alfred	Axel	Bowen	Cato
Alistair	Azariah	Bowie	Cedar
Alonzo	Aziz	Brady	Cedric
Amadeus	Baird	Bram	Charles
Ambrose	Baker	Branch	Charlie
Amias	Balthazar	Brennan	Chase
Amos	Barnaby	Brice	Cheever
Anderson	Bartholomew	Brock	Chester
Angus	Bartleby	Brody	Christo
Ansel	Basie	Brogan	Clancy
Apollo	Basil	Bronson	Clark
Aram	Bastian	Brown	Claude

Clay	Dermot	Evander	Gideon
Clement	Desmond	Everest	Gilbert
Clive	Devlin	Everett	Giulio
Clyde	Dex	Ewan	Gower
Cole	Dexter	Ezekiel	Grady
Colt	Dhani	Ezra	Graham
Colton	Dixon	Farrell	Granger
Conan	Django	Fergus	Gray
Connor	Donovan	Field	Grayson
Conrad	Dougal	Finian	Griffin
Constantine	Drew	Finlay	Grover
Cooper	Drummer	Finn	Gulliver
Corbin	Dudley	Finnegan	Gunther
Cormac	Duff	Fiorello	Gus
Cornelius	Duncan	Fisher	Guthrie
Cosimo	Eamon	Fletcher	Hal
Cosmo	Easton	Flint	Hamish
Crane	Eben	Florian	Hank
Crispin	Edison	Floyd	Hardy
Crosby	Edmund	Flynn	Harrison
Cruz	Edward	Ford	Harry
Cullen	Egan	Forrest	Hart
Curran	Eleazar	Foster	Harvey
Cyprian	Eli	Fox	Hawk
Cyrus	Elias	Francis	Hector
Dalton	Elijah	Frank	Hendrix
Damian	Elio	Fred	Henry
Damon	Ellington	Frederick	Hiram
Dane	Elliot	Fritz	Holden
Daniel	Ellis	Frost	Homer
Darius	Elvis	Gable	Horatio
Darwin	Emilian	Gage	Hudson
Dashiell	Emmanuel	Galway	Hugh
David	Emmett	Gardener	Hugo
Davis	Enzo	Gareth	Humphrey
Dawson	Ephraim	Gatsby	Huxley
Dax	Erasmus	Gavin	Ian
Declan	Ernest	George	Ignatius
Denver	Esau	Giacomo	Indigo

Indio	Kai	Lowell	Nathan
Inigo	Keaton	Loyal	Nathaniel
Innes	Keegan	Luc	Ned
Isaac	Kenyon	Luca	Nehemiah
Isaiah	Kenzo	Lucas	Nelson
Ishmael	Kermit	Lucian	Niall
Isidore	Kiefer	Lucius	Nicholas
Ivor	Kieran	Luke	Nicholson
Jabez	Killian	Lysander	Nico
Jack	Kingston	Mack	Nicolo
Jackson	Knox	Macon	Nile
Jagger	Lachlan	Maddox	Noah
James	Laird	Magnus	Noam
Jared	Langston	Malachi	Noble
Jarvis	Laredo	Malachy	Nolan
Jasper	Lars	Malcolm	North
Jax	Laszlo	Malo	Oak
Jeb	Lazarus	Marco	Obadiah
Jedidiah	Leander	Marcus	Ocean
Jefferson	Leif	Marino	Octavius
Jenson	Lemuel	Marlon	Odin
Jeremiah	Lennon	Martin	Oliver
Jericho	Lennox	Mason	Omar
Jethro	Leo	Matteo	Orion
Joaquin	Leon	Matthias	Orlando
Joe	Leonardo	Max	Orson
Jonah	Leopold	Maximus	Oscar
Jonas	Lev	Mercer	Osias
Joseph	Levi	Micah	Otis
Josiah	Lewis	Miles	Otto
Jubal	Liam	Miller	Owen
Judah	Lincoln	Milo	Painter
Judd	Linus	Moe	Paolo
Jude	Lionel	Morris	Pascal
Jules	Llewellyn	Morrissey	Patrick
Julian	Logan	Moses	Pax
Julius	Lorcan	Moss	Paxton
Jupiter	Lorenzo	Murphy	Penn
Justice and Justus	Louis	Nash	Percival

Percy	Romeo	Taj	Waylon
Peregrine	Ronan	Tarquin	Webb
Perry	Roone	Tate	Webster
Phelan	Rory	Tavish	Wesley
Philip	Roscoe	Tennyson	West
Philo	Rowan	Thaddeus	Weston
Phineas	Roy	Thatcher	Wheeler
Piers	Rudy	Thelonious	Wilder
Pike	Rufus	Theo	Will
Plato	Rupert	Theodore	William
Poe	Ryder	Thomas	Willoughby
Prescott	Samson	Thor	Wilson
Preston	Samuel	Tiberius	Winston
Primo	Saul	Tiernan	Wolf
Prosper	Sawyer	Tierney	Wyatt
Quade	Sayer	Titus	Wylie
Quentin	Seamus	Tobias	Xander
Quincy	Sebastian	Tolliver	Xavier
Quinn	Septimus	Torquil	Zachariah
Rafferty	Seth	Trent	Zan
Ralph	Shaw	Tristan	Zane
Ranger	Shepherd	Truman	Zebadiah
Raphael	Silas	Tucker	Zebedee
Ray	Simeon	Tully	Zebulon
Raymond	Simon	Turner	Zeno
Redmond	Sinjin	Ulysses	Zephyr
Reed	Sky	Urban	Zion
Reeve	Slade	Uri	
Remy	Slater	Valentine	
Reuben	Smith	Victor	
Rex	Solomon	Viggo	
Reynard	Soren	Vincent	
Rhett	Spencer	Virgil	
Rhys	Stellan	Vladimir	
Rio	Stone	Walden	
River	Sullivan	Waldo	
Rocco	Sven	Walker	
Rollo	Sweeney	Walter	
Roman	Sylvester	Watson	

Made in the USA
Lexington, KY
14 May 2014